ARIZONA
An Illustrated History

ILLUSTRATED HISTORIES FROM HIPPOCRENE

Published...

Arizona
Patrick Lavin

Celtic World
Patrick Lavin

China
Yong Ho

England
Henry Weisser

France
Lisa Neal

Greece
Tom Stone

Ireland
Henry Weisser

Israel
David C. Gross

Italy
Joseph F. Privitera

Korea
David Rees

Mexico
Michael Burke

Poland
Iwo Cyprian Pogonowski

Poland in World War II
Andrew Hempel

Russia
Joel Carmichael

Spain
Fred James Hill

Forthcoming...

Cracow
Zdzislaw Zygulski

Egypt
Fred James Hill

Gypsy World
Atanas Slavov

London
Nick Awde & Robert Chester

Moscow
Kathy Murrell

Paris
Elaine Mokhtefi

Portugal
Lisa Neal

Romania
Nicholas Klepper

Sicily
Joseph F. Privitera

Tikal
John Montgomery

Venice
Lisa Neal

Vietnam
Shelton Woods

Wales
Henry Weisser

ARIZONA
An Illustrated History

Patrick Lavin

HIPPOCRENE BOOKS, INC.
New York

All photos herein are courtesy of Marshall Trimble, Director of the Maricopa Community College Southwest Studies Program.

For information, address:
HIPPOCRENE BOOKS, INC.
171 Madison Avenue
New York, NY 10016

Cataloging-in-Publication Data available from the Library of Congress.

Printed in the United States of America.

To Joan Amelia

My anam ċara and wisest counselor

 # ACKNOWLEDGMENTS

I wish to thank the many individuals whose help and encouragement made this book possible. I am especially grateful to my wife Joan for scrutinizing the manuscript and for her encouragement and many creative suggestions, which substantially added to the enhancement and clarity of the text.

I wish to thank Marshall Trimble, director of Maricopa Community College's Southwest Studies, a critically acclaimed author and one of Arizona's most prominent and colorful historians, for his kind permission to let me select from his extensive Arizona photographic collection, the visual documents of events and individuals that I have used in this book.

To edit this work I chose Ann Westlake, an accomplished editor, whose penetrating critique smoothed out the rough edges.

There were others of course who contributed in different ways and I would like to acknowledge their support: the people at Hippocrene Books, particularly Kara Migliorelli and Paul Simpson, my agent Elisabet McHugh, my family, and my friends.

The many historians and writers I consulted will be evident throughout the book and are acknowledged in the bibliography.

TABLE OF CONTENTS

INTRODUCTION

A rizona may be the youngest of the nation's contiguous states, but it is an ancient land that has been inhabited for millenniums. Countless Indians lived in the valleys, canyons, and mountains of the American Southwest, many making their home in Arizona.[1] They began arriving in the Western Hemisphere from Asia thousands of years ago, migrating across the land bridge that existed between Siberia and Alaska and, over the course of time, by one route or another, spreading southward and eastward across the continent. We have little information and can only guess about the ancient cultures, social characteristics, and forms of social organization of these ancient colonists. Prehistoric man left few records other the bones of the large animals he hunted; historians have had to rely almost entirely on archaeological evidence to piece together the obscure roots and living styles of these peoples.

---

1. In the discussion of Native American culture, the Southwest encompasses Arizona, New Mexico, southern Utah, southwestern Nevada, and the California border along the Colorado River.

1

Delineated on the east by the western slopes of the Rocky Mountains, on the north by the largely impenetrable Grand Canyon and Colorado Plateau region, on the south by Mexico's frontier Sonora state, and on the west by the lower Colorado River and Mojave Desert, frontier Arizona presented a formidable barrier for most early travelers, including the cavalcade of tenacious Spanish explorers and missionaries who ventured across the great Southwest from the early 1500s.

Before Columbus discovered America, there were thousands of native residents living in the American Southwest. Many of them lived in the Gila and Santa Cruz Valleys, an area extending from present-day Phoenix to the Mexican border. They were the Anasazi, Hohokam, and Mogollon peoples. The first missionaries came to plant the seeds of Christianity and Spanish culture in this area. While two Franciscan priests, Juan de la Asuncion and Pedro Nadal, are mentioned in some sources as having traveled from Mexico northward to the upper Colorado River in 1538, the first European definitely known to have explored the region was another Franciscan, Fray Marcos de Niza, an Italian in the service of Spain. Early in 1539, de Niza was sent into the northern country by the viceroy of New Spain, Antonio de Mendoza, in order to search for the legendary "Seven Golden Cities of Cibola"—Zuni villages occupying sites near the present town of Gallop, New Mexico. These cities were rumored to have streets and walls paved with gold and precious jewels. Marcos de Niza and his guide,

Esteban the Black Moor, followed a trail that lured them across rugged terrain through present-day Sonora to the headwaters of the San Pedro River, at the confluence of the Gila River. They crossed the Gila, and continued northward until they arrived at the Indian town of Hawikuh, the first of the Zuni pueblos in New Mexico.

The following year, a Spanish expedition under the command of Francisco Vasquez de Coronado set out from Mexico City and headed north across the parched, forbidding Chihuahuan Desert in search of Cibola. Instead of the fabled gold-paved cities, he found Zuni pueblos occupied by subsistence farmers. Coronado, although disappointed at not finding the Seven Golden Cities of Cibola, gave the first clear account of the magnitude of the territory. Exploration soon followed from Zacatecas, a city three hundred miles northwest of Mexico City.

As the missionaries, soldiers, and prospectors pushed northward, they encountered Indians of a different culture from the Aztec-dominated one they had first encountered in Mexico. These peoples, scattered throughout an area bounded on the east by the upper Rio Grande River and on the north and west by the San Juan and Colorado Rivers, shared a simple agricultural economy, with each community independent and self-sufficient. There was trade, to be sure, which extended widely throughout the region, but there was no system of markets to encourage individual or real specialization. Traded goods were rarely of food or basic tools;

luxury and ceremonial items, such as shells, semi-precious stones, and other unique products of localized origins were the items of choice.

Following Coronado's retreat in 1542, it was almost one hundred and fifty years before the Spaniards again showed interest in the territory they had named Pimeria Alta. Eusebio Francisco Kino, known as the legendary padre on horseback, arrived in 1687. For the first six of his twenty-four years in the area, this energetic Jesuit was practically the only white man among the Pimans.[2] Historians depict him as the pioneer, trailblazer, cartographer, organizer, and spiritual director of Pimeria Alta. He founded twenty-nine missions and seventy-three visitas, including missions at San Ignacio, Tubutama, and San Xavier de Bac.

Unlike Coronado and his conquistadors who came for gold, Kino came to spread the word of God. He was a peacemaker, not a warrior; he promoted self-sufficiency among the natives by making them adept at more suitable agriculture techniques. His treks during his missionary interval took him to the absolute limits of Pimeria Alta: from the San Pedro to the Colorado Rivers and from the Concepcion to the Gila. He came upon the Casa Grande ruin and descended the Gila River to its convergence with the Colorado. His feats of endurance are legendary: he is given the credit for pushing back the frontier and paving the way for the

---

2. Native Indian tribes in the region.

4

first white settlements in Arizona. However, the spiritual and temporal work of Kino and his fellow Jesuits was tragically interrupted in 1767. This year saw the Spanish Crown, for political reasons, expel the Jesuit Order from all lands under Spain's dominion, and replace them with the Franciscans.

The sudden demise of the Jesuits' northwest missionary dominion left an extensive sector of the frontier economically and socially disoriented, as the Jesuits had administered Indian affairs for the entire region. Kino's missions soon fell into ruin and were abandoned. Before the Franciscans arrived, the people of the missions had to work for a *comisario* instead of a padre. Spiritual life, such as it was, deteriorated among the mission Indians. Only occasionally did anyone preach to them; for all of Pimeria Alta's 50,000 square miles, there were only two circuit-riding parish priests. The mission Indians lived in mounting fear of Apache attack. The Apaches had not planted crops, because they had been promised assistance in peace treaties with the Spaniards. Consequently, when rumors spread that the Spaniards were reneging on their pledge, the ill-provisioned Indians were determined to take what they could by force.

After the Jesuits departed, the Franciscans moved into Pimeria Alta—the most northern frontier of Sonora. One of their own members, Father Garcia, trekked further west, north, and east than had Fr. Kino. However, rebellious Seris and Yumas ultimately destroyed three of the four mission outposts the Franciscans had established in the area, and the fourth was ceded to the Franciscan province of Jalisco.

Spanish colonization and Christianization efforts in the region, as elsewhere throughout New Spain, continued for more than two hundred years, until the Mexican Revolution ousted the Spaniards in 1821. Throughout the period, Spanish missionaries, military captains, and colonial administrators worked closely in promoting Spanish culture. However, after nearly two centuries of steady advance northward from the Valley of Mexico, the Spanish conquest began to falter during the late 1700s. In the face of the insurgent Apaches, they retreated southward.

Americans began to arrive in the New Mexico settlements after reports of the territory's rich resources spread throughout the East. By 1824, a few bold traders (who had been transporting merchandise over the trail between Independence, Missouri and Santa Fe) pushed their way farther west into the Apache country of Arizona. They explored along the Gila, Salt, and Colorado Rivers, where they found an abundance of beaver and game. After Arizona was acquired from Mexico, the first Americans to venture into the region, up to the end of the eighteenth century, came primarily in search of quick fortunes.

The Territory of Arizona was carved out of the western portion of New Mexico, a vast territory that had been created by the Compromise of 1850 after the

Mexican War, and then had been expanded further by the Gadsden Purchase Treaty in 1854. It was the Organic Act, signed into law by President Lincoln on February 24, 1863, that created the Territory of Arizona. Before its acquisition by the United States, Arizona was under Spanish and Mexican jurisdictions. Present-day southern Arizona was the northern fringe of the Sonoran districts of Fronteras, Arizpe, Magdalena, and Alter. Geographically, politically, and socially, they were interrelated. The very name of the state was taken from a mining district south of the present international boundary—the fabled and fabulous mines of Arizonac.[3] Another forty-nine years would pass before Arizona was granted statehood in 1912. Before it was finally admitted into the Union, wagon roads and railroads had already ushered in a flood of settlers attracted by the lure of its unique life style. During the period of preparation for statehood, Arizona was administered by appointed governors and elected legislatures. It was represented in Congress by nonvoting delegates, the first being Charles Poston—a man often referred to as the "Father" of Arizona because of his role in orchestrating the passage of the Organic Act.[4]

Arizona owes much of its color and individuality to the Mexicans, who largely retain their own culture and customs in an environment constantly growing more

3. Kieran McCarty, *Desert Documentary* (1976).
4. Jay J. Wagoner, *Arizona Territory 1863–1912* (1980).

Americanized. Almost every city and town of any size has its Mexican quarter. Most Mexicans are a fusion of Spanish and Indian blood and proud of their ancestry. History is filled with the names of Mexicans who played a prominent part in the development of the first settlements. Their descendants are prominent and respected citizens. Arizona's foremost hero in World War II was a Mexican American, Sylvestre Herrera, who was awarded the Congressional Medal of Honor by President Harry Truman for single-handedly holding back an enemy attack from pinning down his unit.

The Southwest Indians, with their varied cultures and much-valued art, add richness and diversity to life in Arizona. Many young Indian men have distinguished themselves fighting in the services of the United States. In World War II, when the Japanese army was intercepting Allied messages and creating turmoil with deceptive information, Navajo Indians perfected a special code using their native language, which the Japanese could not intercept. The legacy of one Piman Indian is immortalized in the Iwo Jima war memorial in Washington, D.C. Ira Hayes, an Ackimoel O'odham Indian from the Gila River Reservation near Phoenix, was one of six marines photographed raising the American flag atop a small dormant volcano on the Japanese-held island of Iwo Jima on February 23, 1945. For days, he and his fellow marines had fought bravely to capture the island. Although the battle was still raging, the heroic performance of Ira and the

Ira Hayes, a Pima Indian from Bapchule, was one of the marines who raised the flag at Iwo Jima on February 23, 1945.

others served to reassure the marines fighting on the hillsides and the beaches below that victory was close at hand.

From the pioneering treks of seventeenth-century Spanish conquistadors into the early part of the twentieth century, Arizona was looked upon as a barren hostile land, the barrier that had to be traversed before reaching the "promised land" of California. However, twentieth-century technology changed that awful image forever when massive irrigation projects and air conditioning made the desert acceptable for habitation year-round. World War II transformed the nation's sixth largest state into a huge military-industrial complex. After the war, other technology companies moved their operations to the state. Since the 1950s, Arizona has become one of the most desired places to live in the United States.[5]

---

5. Marshall Trimble, *Arizona: A Cavalcade of History* (1990).

1 LAND OF CONTRASTS

> The popular conception of Arizona is of an
> unfertile desert country, yet the flora ranges
> from the subtropical to the sub-alpine.
> —from the *WPA Guide to 1930s Arizona*

Arizona is an awesome land where towering mountain peaks stand guard over unrivaled wilderness, and where one will find the most remarkable mix of deserts in the world. The four distinct deserts that make up the great North American Deserts—Chihuahuan, Mojave, Great Basin, and Sonoran—converge within the state. No other region in North America offers such a broad range of life zones, as well as the native plants, animals, and people that inhabit them. Five of the world's six principal biotech communities can be found on the Santa Catalina Mountains—a single, mountainous "sky island" emerging out of the floor of the lower Sonoran Desert near Tucson, where summer monsoons and deep winter snows dump precious moisture, bringing life to the harsh deserts below [6]

---

6. John Annerino, *Adventuring in Arizona* (1996).

The Sonoran Desert, the southern one-third of the state, is one of the most unique landscapes in the world. A wide variety of desert plants grapple for the sparse rainfall that amounts, in some parts, to less than three inches per year. Here the Chihuahuan Desert overlaps the southeastern part of the state, while the Mojave Desert overlaps the northwestern corner.

Arizona, with its 113,956 square miles of territory, ranks as the sixth largest state in the union. Utah lies along the full extent of its extreme northern boundary, as does Mexico along the southern border. Arizona's eastern and western borders are New Mexico and California and Nevada, respectively. Arizona comprises three distinctive physical areas, each with its own individual climate, flora, and fauna. The northern section, particularly in the northeast, contains lofty plateaus gashed by huge canyons; in the central section, high mountain ranges extend diagonally in a general northwest-southwest direction; the southern section consists largely of low and level river plains in the east, and of a great desert traversed by the Gila River in the west.

An area of approximately 45,000 square miles lies within the Colorado Plateau region, which is distinguished by its remarkable canyons, including the Grand Canyon of the Colorado River. Two immense contrasting forces—volcanic and erosive—have played important parts in determining the physical characteristics of the area.[7] The San Francisco Plateau, the portion of the Grand Canyon region lying south of the Colorado River, comprises two to three thousand square miles, with Flagstaff near its center. The region is covered with lava flows and dotted with several hundred volcanic cones.

Above the surrounding tableland rise the San Francisco Mountains with Humphery Peak, an extinct volcano that is the highest point in Arizona at 12,611 feet. From the base of the plateau, there is a rapid descent to the south. The area is drained by the Colorado, Little Colorado, and Verde Rivers, together with a number of smaller streams. The northeastern section is a canyon-cut, broken tableland studded with hills, buttes, and mesas; the average elevation is about five thousand feet. One of the most interesting features is the Painted Desert, a wild plateau destitute of water and vegetation, whose surface is broken by columns, as well as by individual peaks and buttes of remarkably colored sandstone that has been eroded into fantastic shapes. The famous Petrified Forest is within this desert.

Lying between the plateau and plains sections is the mountain region, comprising the lower half of Mojave County; all of Yavapai, Gila, Greenlee, Graham, Cochise, and Santa Cruz Counties; the western half of Pima and Pinal Counties; and the northwestern part of

---

7. *WPA Guide to 1930s Arizona* (1940).

Maricopa County. The general elevation of the entire area is higher than that of the plains district, but lower than that of the Colorado Plateau. This region is part of the Mexican Highland division and contains thirty mountain chains of the Basin and Range type. The peaks are generally from about 4,000 to 6,000 feet above the valley bottoms; several summits, however, rise to elevations of approximately 11,000 feet. The region is rich in mineral resources: principally gold, silver, and copper. The broad ridge that forms the edge of the Colorado Plateau narrows in this mountain region to the Mogollon Rim, and along this ridge stands a great unbroken stretch of pine forest.

The Plains District, comprising about thirty-five percent of the state's area, lies partly in central, but mostly in southern Arizona. The district is well irrigated and contains the Gila and Salt River Valleys—two of the most fertile areas in Arizona. The greater part of the southwestern section, lying within the Sonoran Desert, has a comparatively low elevation. It consists largely of vast stretches of desert plains broken by short mountain chains from 1,000 to 3,000 feet in height, which trend in a northwesterly or south-easterly direction. The mountains are seldom forested, and the plains and broad level valleys maintain characteristic desert flora or are destitute of vegetation.

Most important of Arizona's rivers is the Colorado, which flows through the northwestern part of the state and forms the state's western boundary for nearly all its remaining course. It has many tributaries, chief of which are the Gila, Little Colorado, and Williams Rivers. Along its upper course within Arizona is the magnificent Grand Canyon. The Gila, the second largest river, crosses the state from east to west and flows into the Colorado near Yuma. Its most important tributary is the Salt River, formed by a union of the Black and White Rivers in the Mogollon Mountains. Another of the Gila's tributaries, the Santa Cruz, is in flow only at flood time. The Verde River, a tributary of the Salt, has its source in a series of springs in Chino Valley in the great Colorado Plateau. The Little Colorado rises in the Sierra Blanca Range near the eastern boundary of Arizona— only a short distance from the San Francisco, Black, and Salt Rivers—and enters the Colorado at the Grand Canyon. Most of its course is northwesterly. The Little Colorado's most important tributary is the Zuni River; farther along its course, it is joined by the Rio Puerco and then Lithodendron Creek, on the banks of which is the Petrified Forest.

The Tucson Basin is rich in plant and animal life. The variety of plants ranges from desert grasses and scrub trees to piñon and ponderosa pine forests on the mountain sides, and from cacti on the desert floor to cottonwood and willow along the streams. The varied vegetation supports an equally varied animal life, from desert reptiles and rodents to deer and mountain sheep.

Five mountain ranges enclose the Tucson Basin. The Sierritas and Tucsons form the southern and western boundaries; the Santa Catalina, Rincon, and Santa Rita Mountains make up the northern, eastern, and southern boundaries. The Tucsons and Sierritas are typical low Basin and Range Province Mountains, formed by volcanism and the fracturing of the earth's surface layers. The Catalinas, Rincons, and Santa Ritas, however, are high, massive, and eroded remnants of underground intrusions of granite rock. Their pine-covered summits receive twenty to twenty-five inches of rainfall annually, or three times the average for the Sonoran Desert. Rainfall in the Tucson Basin is also high in comparison to the major portion of the desert—eleven inches annually in contrast to just seven.

Before the expansion of Tucson and the overuse of ground water, precipitation maintained a high water table and a healthy natural environment. Now the local streams flow only occasionally and are entrenched in deep channels. As recently as the late 1800s, the streams flowed on the surface and, by means of ditches, provided water to irrigate crops grown in the flood-plain. Reports of the Tucson Basin written between 1700 and 1870 mention that the rivers flowed year-round; that cotton-wood and mesquite grew along their banks; and in some places, beavers built their dams.

Arizona is a fascinating land of lofty mountains, spectacular canyons, ponderosa forests, living deserts, great rivers, mighty dams, broad mesas, mines, ranches, farms, and orchards—a land of contrasts and contradictions, never fully understood, but forever loved by those who know the state.

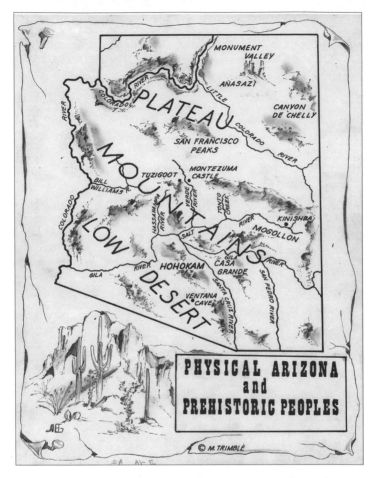

Physical Arizona and Prehistoric People. The so-called Paleo-Indians that peopled prehistoric Arizona probably arrived about 11,000 years ago, after a long journey from Asia.

2 PRE-EUROPEAN PEOPLES

Arizona's native peoples present an astonishing contrast: differing as much in religion, physical appearance, culture, and lifestyle as do the peoples of Europe.

Starting thousands of years ago, Asiatic people began migrating across the Bering Strait onto the American Continent and, over time, worked their way southward and eastward. According to archaeological findings, Arizona has been inhabited anywhere from twelve to fifteen thousand years—an estimate at best, as prehistoric man left few records from which to make an accurate assessment.

The first known inhabitants of the Southwest are referred to, in archaeological terms, as *Paleo-Indians* (the "ancient ones"), who dwelt here from unknown times to *c.* 6000 B.C. They were mammoth hunters and, as the environment changed and the big game they hunted moved eastward, they followed. As they withdrew, bands from the California desert regions and from northern Mexico moved into the areas they vacated. Over the next four thousand or so years, a new culture evolved—distinguished as Desert People. The folks of this culture gathered and hunted for their food supply, and somewhere between 3000 and 2500 B.C. introduced *maize* (Indian corn) as a supplement for their diet. These Desert People were the link between the ancient mammoth hunters and the prehistoric Anasazi, Hohokam, Mogollon, Patayan, Salado, and Sinagua. Because many of their sites have been located in Cochise territory, these desert dwellers are grouped together as the Cochise People.

Anasazi Culture

Archaeologists tell us that the Anasazi entered the Four Corners area about 200 B.C. Dubbed "Basket-makers" because of the delicate storage baskets they made from yucca fibers, they had evolved from a nomadic to a sedentary lifestyle by 500 A.D., cultivating crops of corn, beans, and squash. About 700 A.D., they moved out of their caves into pit houses—cone-shaped, one-roomed structures sunk three to five feet in the ground. In time, these round houses gave way to compact apartment-type dwellings with common walls, which the Spaniards referred to as pueblos. Some were quite enormous. For example, Pueblo Bonito in Chaco Canyon (New Mexico) was five stories high and had over eight hundred compartments. According to sources, its peak population may have surpassed one thousand.

A major change took place among the Anasazi sometime around 1050 A.D. They relocated to the tops of mesas and into the cliffs, where they built large cliff dwellings. Today, one can visit these cliff dwellings at Navajo National Monument and Keet Seel, the largest and one of the best preserved in the Southwest. Three hundred years later, during the zenith of their culture, the Anasazi hastily abandoned these magnificent dwellings. Archaeologists disagree over what caused this to happen. Some believe a catastrophic 23-year drought from 1276 to 1299 A.D. was the cause. Others claim that warfare—either from within the Anasazi culture, or from outside invaders—brought about their downfall.

Mogollon Culture

The Mogollon culture evolved out of the Cochise culture and came into its own about 300 B.C. A mountain people living on wild game, nuts, and berries, they ranged across the mountains of eastern Arizona, southwestern New Mexico, and northern Mexico in the region that later became known as Apacheria. Their homes were usually one-room pit houses constructed of twigs, logs, and branches covered with mud. Unlike the Anasazi who lived in "condo-style" dwellings, the

21

Mogollon were a village people who lived in single-family units widely spread along a ridge that overlooked their fields. The decline of the Mogollon culture occurred in the late 1200s A.D., about the same time as the Anasazi. As with the Anasazi, archaeologists attribute their exit to invaders or drought or both, and believe that they migrated to the Casa Grandes area of Chihuahua, Mexico.

Hohokam Culture

In the Sonoran Desert area of southern Arizona there lived a highly developed civilization that would last for seventeen hundred years before it also collapsed. They were the Hohokams—a present-day Pima Indian word meaning the "Ancient ones." This agricultural society migrated into southern Arizona from Mexico around 300 B.C. and settled in villages along the Salt and Gila Rivers. By 200 A.D., they had moved into the Tucson Basin and established communities along the Santa Cruz and Rillito Rivers. To grow crops in desert conditions, they modified their farming methods with a cleverly-engineered canal irrigation system—a system that would serve as a model for twentieth-century irrigation projects in the area. Archaeologists have traced nearly one hundred miles of canals around Florence and up to one hundred and thirty-five in the Phoenix area.

An artist's conception of Hohokam farmers about
1100 A.D., from a painting by Charles O. Kemper.
(PHOTO: SALT RIVER PROJECT ARCHIVES)

Diorama of Hohokam farmers digging a canal in the desert of southern Arizona. (PHOTO: SALT RIVER PROJECT ARCHIVES)

Archaeologist Emil Haury, who has studied the Hohokam culture extensively, called them the "First masters of the American Desert." Many have marveled at their developed society and the mammoth structures that they built in such a harsh environment. Their origins lay with the archaic hunter-gatherers who lived in Arizona for several thousand years, but the Hohokam drew from Mesoamerican civilization as well. A distinct Hohokam culture was in place along the Gila and Salt Rivers and their tributaries by 300 A.D. Like other southwestern farming peoples, they lived in permanent settlements, made pottery, and traded. Their main crops were corn, beans, squash, tobacco, and cotton. They formed irrigation communities along the main canals. In areas without perennial streams, they tapped groundwater or diverted storm runoff into dry-land fields.

With the onset of what is referred to as the Classic period (around 1150 A.D.), Hohokams began to withdraw from outlying settlements and concentrate in large villages. Pithouses surrounding central plazas gave way to walled compounds. Casa Grande, the most impressive of the Hohokam structures, stands on the south bank of the Gila River near Coolidge. On the north side of the Salt River, on the edge of Phoenix airport, is Pueblo Grande, a house structure eclipsed in size and grandeur only by Casa Grande. Archaeologists tell us that mirrors and copper bells taken from excavations at Casa Grande reveal a link to tropical Mexico, as do the shallow, oval

Casa Grande Ruins. (PHOTO: BUEHMAN HARTWELL)

pits found in major villages. These oval pits may have been arenas for ball games like the Aztecs played, or they may have been gathering places unrelated to sports. Archaeologists believe that a declining popularity of ball-courts in the twelfth century denotes a gradual shift in the Hohokam world.

Sometime around 1400–1425 A.D., the Hohokam mysteriously disappeared. An epidemic may have wiped them out. The prevailing theory, however, is that alkalization of the soil caused by centuries of irrigation had made the land useless, forcing them to migrate elsewhere to survive. Where did they go after they left the

Gila watershed, where they had survived for seventeen hundred years? It is believed that they migrated south, probably out of Arizona and into the valleys of Mexico—a claim that cannot be traced or substantiated. At the time of their disappearance, they would have numbered 15,000 or more.

When Father Eusebio Kino and his party of missionaries visited Casa Grande in 1694, they found only the empty shell of the once-flourishing village. The only people living near it were a few communities of Pima Indians whose standard of living was in no way comparable to that of their Hohokam predecessors. They referred to the site as belonging to the Hohokams, "the ancient ones."

Other Pre-Historic Cultures

While Anasazi, Hohokam, and Mogollon are considered the major prehistoric cultures of Arizona, there were also three smaller cultures: Patayan, Salado, and Sinagua. The Sinagua arrived c. 500 A.D. in the Flagstaff-Verde Valley area, where they lived in cliffs and in stone villages around the San Francisco Mountains. They remained here until the eruption of Sunset Crater in 1064. Later, they returned and farmed the region, building several pueblos, the largest being Wupatki. Another dwelling was Montezuma Castle, a striking twenty-room apartment-style building nestled beneath

The Wupatki Ruins between Flagstaff and the Painted Desert. (PHOTO: GARY M. JOHNSON)

Montezuma Castle Cliff Dwelling. (PHOTO: BUEHMAN HARTWELL)

an overhang above Beaver Creek. Tuzigoot, the ruins of another Sinagua pueblo, was built on a hilltop overlooking the Verde River near Clarkdale. After the long drought in the latter part of the thirteenth century, the Sinagua migrated or went into decline. Some suggest they may have moved to the mesas alongside the Hopi.

The Salado, distant kin to the Anasazi, lived in cliff villages along the Salt River. They mysteriously vanished and may have been assimilated by the larger Hohokam and Mogollon cultures.

The Patayan lived in the Prescott area, west of Flagstaff, and along the Colorado River in western Arizona, where they farmed, hunted, and scavenged for wild berries. They also vanished, leading some to believe that they evolved into the Yuma-language people of western Arizona.

Contemporary Arizona Indian Tribes

Before the Europeans arrived, Arizona belonged to the Native Americans. They were the true pioneers: tilling the first fields, building the first communities, and constructing the first irrigation canals. When the Spaniards arrived, most of the tribes were still living in the Stone Age. Arizona's natives had not learned to make tools of metal, and the only domestic animals they raised were the dog and the turkey. The wheel was unfamiliar and the bow-and-arrow was the most advanced weaponry.[8] Supplemented by gathering wild fruits and nuts and some hunting, agriculture was the mainstay for human survival.

Within a half-century of Columbus' landing in the New World, the Native Americans of the Southwest were subject to the first series of conquests. The course of the area's Indian cultures was forever altered with the arrival of the Spaniards. Through three centuries, the Spaniards sought to educate and indoctrinate the natives in Spanish culture and the teachings of the Catholic Church. Spanish withdrawal from the Southwest in the early nineteenth century was followed by a period of exceptionally rapid change and upheaval for many Indian communities in Arizona. Within a generation after the Gadsden Purchase in 1854, Anglo-Americans moved forcibly into different parts of the region to exert dominance over the native inhabitants. The events of this traumatic period in nineteenth-century Arizona history are well publicized in episodes such as the Long Walk of the Navajos, the Camp Grant massacre, and the Apache wars.

Along with the final defeat and confinement of Indians on reservations, came "Americanization" through a protraction of federal programs that had a profound and lasting influence upon Indian individuals, communities, and entire tribes. The gradual ending of the American frontier and the growing commercial

8. Bert M. Fireman, *Arizona: Historic Land* (1982).

interests in Arizona often threatened the very existence of the reservations, as American ranchers and farmers vied for more and more of the area's grazing land and water supply. Today, while Indian reservations occupy approximately one-fourth of Arizona land, much of it is of poor grazing quality.

Arizona's contemporary Indian population is somewhat above two hundred and fifty thousand. The tribes present as striking a contrast among themselves as does the land on which they reside: differing in language, physical appearance, religion, culture, and lifestyle. Because many Indian communities are far removed from urban areas, they have been able to retain their culture and traditions.

Hopi

The Hopi communities of present-day Arizona and New Mexico are probably the two oldest surviving communities of the Pueblo people. Believed to have descended from the ancient Anasazi, the Hopi call themselves Hopitu, meaning the "Peaceful People." The first Europeans to visit them were soldiers from Coronado's expedition in 1540, during his quest for the mythical Seven Golden Cities of Cibola. The Franciscans, against the wishes of Hopi leaders, opened a mission among them in 1629. However, the Spanish were driven out in the Great Revolt in 1680, at which time four missionaries were killed and the church destroyed. During the next two hundred years, the Hopi survived drought, smallpox, and raids from the Ute, Apache, and Navajo. During the "Americanization" period, Hopi children were forced to attend schools far away from Hopiland.

The Hopi have a complicated, interwoven social structure: each village is a separate entity, each individual has a particular responsibility, and each clan is designated for particular duties. Land among the Hopi is communal, given to the clans and apportioned to the various families to use and hand down to their daughters. They are a matrilineal society, and although a man marries and lives with his wife near her clan, he still has responsibility to his own clan mother. Women own the home, gardens, and pueblo furnishings; men, on the other hand, take care of herding, farming, and activities away from the village. Ownership of such property as livestock belongs to the male members, a custom adopted from the Spanish.

A deeply religious people, their lives center around the kiva, an underground ceremonial chamber, where ceremonies are conducted for long life, healing, rain, and fertility. The high point of the year is August, when the snake-dance ceremony is performed. Life has not been greatly affected by contemporary civilization and the time-honored Hopi way continues to survive today.

Hopi Indian girls grinding corn: a home scene at Shonghopavi c. 1903.

Apache

Historically, the Apache have been the most warlike of the Arizona tribes. Akin to the Navajo, they migrated from the Great Plains into the areas that are now Arizona, New Mexico, and northern Mexico about 1100 A.D. Around 1400, various bands went off in different directions. The Navajo and Jicarilla Apache settled in the San Juan River Basin of the Four Corners. The Mescalero Apache relocated to southern New Mexico; the Lipan and Kiowa bands wandered across Texas; the Chiricahua settled in northern Mexico, southern Arizona, and southwestern New Mexico; and what became known as the western Apache were drawn to the rugged central mountains of Arizona.

For some three hundred years, the Apache held the Spanish and Mexican intrusions into Arizona to the area below the Gila River. Only a few interlopers dared penetrate into the land that was called "Apacheria." Quoting Marshall Trimble, it was left to the ambitious Americans to make the final conquest of Apacheria; and it would take some twenty-five years of tough guerrilla warfare to accomplish the feat.

The Apache believe in a supreme being called *Usen*, who is the giver of all life. *Usen* is of no sex or location, and it can only be approached through a medium. Each Apache has his own medium, which is his guardian spirit. The medicine man is a powerful

Apache Warrior.

"Na-buash-I-ta"—Apache Medicine Man.
(PHOTO: BEN WITTICK)

influence among the Apache, even to this day. Many place more trust in the medicine man than in the Indian tribal leaders, whom they feel have been greatly swayed by the white man and his institutions. Traditionally, the Apache practiced polygamy; the shortage of males in this warrior society made this necessary.

Today, some twenty thousand Apache occupy the White Mountain and San Carlos Reservations in one of the most scenic spots in Arizona. They own large numbers of cattle and, as one writer describes it, "In an ironic twist, Apache have become cowboys complete with addiction to rodeos and pickup trucks."

Navajo

The Navajo, like the Apache to whom they are closely related, are believed to have migrated in the 1400s into the Four Corners area, where they adopted many of the customs of the Pueblo people. Before the Spaniards introduced sheep, cattle, and horses in the sixteenth century, the Navajo were a small tribe eking out a living from cultivation, which was supplemented by hunting, raiding, and gathering. They have been described as great borrowers: silversmithing from the Spanish, weaving and sheep-raising from the Hopi, and hell-raising from the Utes. However, their earth-covered houses have remained unchanged and can be traced back to their Asian origin.

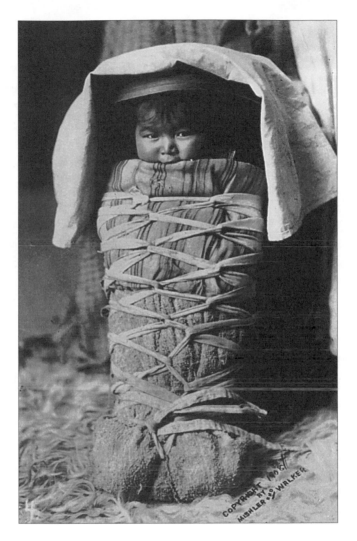

Navajo Indian baby in a cradleboard.

For more than three hundred years, the Navajo battled their traditional enemies—the Comanche and the Utes. They fought a long series of raid and counter-raid wars with the Spanish, and later with the Mexicans, along the Rio Grande. When the American Army occupied Navajo traditional lands in 1846, it was to assist local settlers along the Rio Grande to bring an end to the Navajo raids. For a time, nothing much was done to bring them into submission. Finally, the legendary mountain-man-turned-soldier Kit Carson rounded up eight thousand Navajo and drove them like cattle on the infamous three-hundred-mile walk from Canyon de Chelly to Bosque Redondo, New Mexico. In 1863, the Navajo were relocated along the Pecos River, where two years later a smallpox epidemic took the lives of some two thousand. A treaty was negotiated in 1868 between the tribe and the federal government, allowing the Navajo to return to their beloved Four Corners. Today, on some fifteen thousand plus square miles of mostly barren land, the Navajo live in widely scattered hogans (houses) and make their living raising sheep and cultivating crops.

There are many customs and taboos among the Navajo: the door of the hogan must always face east; the Navajo must never kill a snake or a coyote; they must never eat bear meat; a man must never look at, or speak to, his mother-in-law and must observe this taboo even though he lives near her. When a person dies inside the hogan, the body is removed through a hole cut in the north wall. The hogan is then never used again. The spirits or ghosts that inhabit a hogan where someone has died are called *chindis*. One does not call out the dead person's name for fear the chindi might respond to the call.

Today, there are 200,000 Navajo inhabiting northeastern Arizona. Economically, they are much better off than were their ancestors. Their reservation produces more energy than elsewhere in the state, coal being the primary source. The tribe receives millions of dollars annually in royalties from mining leases.

Havasupai

The Havasupai, a tribe of about six hundred, live in Supai Village at the bottom of Cataract Canyon within Grand Canyon National Park. All supplies, including mail, are brought in by horse and mule train. It is believed that they have lived in the same area since 1100 A.D. They keep no livestock but grow crops of corn, beans, and squash, and supplement their diets with gathering and hunting. Throughout the growing season, they live in the village; when the harvest is gathered, they leave the Canyon for seasonal camps on the plateau, where much of the time is devoted to gathering seeds and hunting small game. They mingle freely with the Hualapai.

41

Hualapai

The Hualapai, kinfolk to the Havasupai, occupy a vast area south of the Grand Canyon. On a few small cultivable areas near streams and springs, they grow crops of corn, squash, and beans. To supplement their diets, they hunt small game and gather berries, fruits, and nuts.

They were first contacted by the Spaniards in 1776, when Father Francisco Garcés visited the area. The next contact occurred fifty years later (1826), when parties of French and American trappers passed through their area. When deposits of rich ore were discovered in the Cerbat and Hualapai Mountains in the 1860s, it attracted large numbers of prospectors and miners—a situation that led to hostilities between the Indians and the interlopers. The tribe's members were gathered up and settled on the Hualapai Reservation in northwest Arizona in 1869, where some fifteen hundred currently live.

Mojave

The Mojave were once the largest and most warlike of all Colorado River Tribes. They lived along both sides of the Colorado River between Needles and Black Canyon, near today's Hoover Dam. They cultivated crops—squash, corn, melons, and beans—and supplemented their diet by hunting small game and gathering mesquite beans and nuts. Early Spanish explorers were in contact with them, but no missions or settlements were set up on

Mojave soil. Mountain men Jed Smith, Ewing Young, and James Ohio Pattie were the first Americans to meet with them. The visits were generally friendly until 1827, when Jed Smith's party was ambushed and nearly wiped out by an angry mob of Mojaves. It was said that the tribe members were smarting over an earlier shoot-out with a different party of trappers.

Today, some eight hundred Mojave live at the Fort Mojave Reservation west of Kingman. Others share the Colorado River Reservation south of Parker, and about three hundred live on the outskirts of Needles.

Chemehuevi

The Chemehuevi are relative newcomers to Arizona, arriving from the Mojave Desert in the early 1800s. They took up residence along the Colorado River, on a spot where the Mojave had earlier driven out a branch of the Maricopa. After settling along the river, they adopted customs similar to those of other local tribes. Today, about five hundred Chemehuevi reside on the Colorado River Reservation, which they share with other tribes.

Yavapai

A Yuma-speaking people, the Yavapai inhabited the rugged region from the Salt River Canyon to the Bradshaw Mountains. They lived in small bands, hunting and gathering nuts and berries. They were akin to the Hualapai and Havasupai in their customs and language, but their close contact with Tonto Apache caused them to adopt many Apache cultural traits. After the winter campaign of 1872–1873, they were placed on a reservation near Fort Verde. Later, they were moved to the San Carlos Reservation east of Globe. Twenty-five years later, they were offered their own reservation at old Fort McDowell on the Verde River northeast of Phoenix. Only two hundred chose to move, the others preferring to remain among the Apache. Today, their population is about one thousand, dispersed on reservations at Fort McDowell, Prescott, and Camp Verde.

Ackimoel O'odham (Pima)

The Ackimoel O'odham—meaning "River People"—may have descended from the Hohokam. For hundreds of years, they have farmed the Gila and Salt River Valleys. Historically, Pima clans were patriarchal. Tribal organization was strong; each village had a chief, and one head chief, elected by the village chiefs, presided over all the villages. Polygamy was practiced. Marshall Trimble relates an amusing story about a chief with several wives who was visited by Senator Carl Hayden, when the latter was sheriff of Maricopa County.[9] It

---

9. Marshall Trimble, *Arizona: A Cavalcade of History* (1990).

seems that a women's group in Phoenix had complained to the sheriff about the chief's polygamous lifestyle, and were pushing him to do something about it. During his visit to the chief, Sheriff Hayden broached the sensitive matter of polygamy, urging him to consider giving up all his wives but one. After much discussion about the subject, the chief finally agreed to accede to the sheriff's demand on one condition: that Hayden choose which wives had to leave and then tell them. Not wishing to involve himself in this complex family affair, Hayden mounted his horse and rode back to Phoenix. Today, the Ackimoel O'odham number about fifteen thousand and are one of the few tribes living near a metropolitan area (Phoenix).

Tohono O'odham (Papago)

According to Spicer, after the Gadsden Purchase, it was the incoming Anglo-Americans that began making the distinction between the Indians who lived on the Gila River—whom they called "Pimas"—and those who lived farther south in the vicinity of Tucson and westward, whom they began referring to as "Papagos."[10] The Papagos, or Tohono O'odham (meaning "Desert People"), are economically the poorest people in the Southwest. Their reservation runs south from below

---

10. Edward H. Spicer, *Cycles of Conquest* (1997).

the Gila River all the way to the Mexican border. When the Spaniards arrived they were raising crops of beans, corn, and squash. Presently, some twenty thousand Tohono O'odham live on reservations in southern Arizona: Ak-Chin near Maricopa, San Xavier near Tucson, and Papago-Gila Bend near Gila Bend.

Cocopah

For centuries the Cocopah planted their crops along the Colorado River below Yuma. The first contact with Europeans was in 1540. Captain Hernando Alarcon anchored his ship at the mouth of the Colorado and went upriver by small boat. Other Spanish explorers, including Padres Kino and Garcés, visited their villages over the next two hundred and fifty years. Fewer than one thousand currently live on a reservation near Yuma.

Maricopa

The Maricopa are related to the Yuman tribes of the Colorado. As they were constantly fighting with them, however, the Maricopa allied with the Pimas in later times. The lifestyle of the Maricopa was similar to other river tribes: growing corn, beans, melons, and cotton, and supplementing their diet by gathering and hunting. They are best known for their beautiful mesquite-fired red pottery. There are now fewer than seven hundred residing with the Pima on reservations near Phoenix: about half live north of Mesa along the Salt River; the other half reside in the West Valley near Tolleson.

Other Tribes

Among several other tribes in Arizona are the Kaibab Paiute, a small semi-nomadic group of hunters and gatherers who live on the Kaibab Reservation at Pipe Spring National Monument.

The Yaqui, the only "non-native" Indians in Arizona, arrived in southern Arizona in the 1880s from Mexico. Yaqui villages are found today in Pascua and Barrio Libre in Tucson; in Guadalupe near Tempe; and in Vista del Camino in Scottsdale.

Yet another tribe, the Quechans, reside at the Fort Yuma Reservation. Until they were forced onto the reservation, they were a fierce, warlike people who stubbornly resisted interlopers traveling over the Gila Trail to California. Fewer than two thousand remain.

THE SPANIARDS ARRIVE

It was every conquistador's dream to find and conquer another Mexico as Cortez had successfully done.

The first Europeans to set foot in what is present-day Arizona were the Spaniards. They arrived before the middle of the 1500s, their lust for gold whetted by the conquest of Mexico by Cortez. Some accounts credit one of Cortez's lieutenants, Jose de Basconales, with having traversed the region as far north as Zuni early in 1525. Two Franciscan priests, Juan de la Asuncion and Pedro Nadal, are mentioned in some sources as having traveled from Mexico northward to the upper Colorado River in 1538; but the first European certainly known to have explored the region that is now Arizona was another Italian Franciscan in the service of Spain, Marcos de Niza. In 1539 he was sent from Mexico City into the "northern country" by the viceroy of New Spain, Antonio de Mendoza, in order to search for the legendary "Seven Golden Cities of

Cibola."[11] These cities were rumored to have streets and walls paved with gold and precious jewels.

It was every conquistador's dream to find and conquer another Mexico as Cortez had successfully done. Rumors abounded, some from European fables, others from the natives' own imaginations: a sea passage called the Strait of Anian, which allegedly led directly to the Indies; the Island of Pearls; another island where gold was the only metal; and perhaps the fabled Seven Lost Cities of Antilla lay somewhere in the vast northland. The myth of Antilla was constantly on the Spaniards' minds when they arrived in the New World.

The story centers on seven bishops who, with their followers, fled the oncoming Moors in 1150 A.D. and sailed west across the Ocean Sea[12] to a place where each bishop established a city that became fabulously wealthy—streets paved with gold, houses made of silver, and walls studded with rubies and emeralds. It so happened that this mythical tale harmonized with the 1536 tale of the discovery of seven golden cities farther to the north, raising hopes that these seven cities, which the Indians called Cibola, were the fabled Seven Cities of Antilla.

The legend of Cibola originated with four survivors of a shipwreck that wandered into the Mexican village of Culiacan in 1536. These survivors endured an eight-year-long odyssey that supposedly took them from the

11. Zuni villages located near the present town of Gallop, New Mexico.
12. Atlantic Ocean.

50

beaches of Florida to as far west as the San Pedro River in present-day Arizona, then southward across the Chihuahuan Desert, over the craggy Sierra Madre Range, and down the Pacific Coast. They then arrived at the northern frontier of the province of Nueva Galicia in the viceroyalty of New Spain, as Mexico was then called. The four—Cabeza de Vaca, Castillo de Maldonado, Dorantes de Carranza, and his slave Esteban—described their incredible trek across the American Continent, as well as the tales of "great cities" that lay to the north, which they occasionally heard from Indians along the way. In an age when superstition prevailed over worldly wisdom, it was easy to find support for the idea that Cibola might be the Seven Lost Cities of Antilla. And the fact that there were "seven" made the story more convincing; surely these must be the Seven Cities of Antilla.[13]

As one might expect, the rumor spread fast and Don Antonio de Mendoza, viceroy in Mexico City, was rapturous at the incredible news of the seven fabulous pueblos with gold-plated walls and turquoise-studded doors. Described as a crafty man, his first move was to purchase the slave Esteban from his master, de Carranza (who was returning to Spain), foreseeing his usefulness in locating Cibola. He then settled on sending a discreet survey party rather than a full-scale expedition, instructing them to report back to him only. Of

13. Alex Shoumatoff, *Legends of the American Desert* (1997).

course the slave could not head the expedition, so de Mendoza selected as leader Fray Marcos de Niza, a Franciscan who had a lot of frontier experience and who was skilled in celestial navigation and astronomy.

Setting out from Mexico City, de Niza and his party reached Compostela in December 1538, where they were welcomed by the new governor of Nueva Galicia, Francisco Vasquez de Coronado. From Compostela, de Niza followed ancient, well-worn trading trails through the land of the Tepehuano and the Opata.[14] At the Sinaloa River one of his party, Fray Onorato, fell sick and had to be taken back to Culiacan. The others proceeded onward, fording the Fuerte River. Fray Marcus was beginning to run out of steam, and at the Mayo, the next big river north of the Fuerte, he decided to let Esteban go on ahead with instructions to send back a messenger with a palm-high cross if he ran into anything important. In the meantime, de Niza crossed the Rio Mayo and reached the Indian village of Vacapa, where he awaited news from Esteban. Four days after they separated, a messenger bearing a large cross arrived with the announcement that Esteban was on his way to the Seven Lost Cities of Cibola, the first of which was only thirty days off.

It is thought that Esteban and his party trekked northward for four days to a Tepehuano village, where the four survivors had previously stopped on their

---

14. Ibid.

journey, and had curiously named the Town of Hearts. Esteban's party continued on for two weeks through the uninhabited cactus country of southern Arizona, passing near the future sites of Huachuca and Tombstone, until they arrived at the first of the seven cities—actually a Zuni pueblo called Hawikuh. What happened when the party arrived is not clear, but it appears that Esteban ignored the Zuni's warning not to enter the village. The Zuni attacked, capturing and killing all but three of Esteban's party. According to some sources, Esteban's body was dismembered and pieces were sent to each of the seven pueblos as proof that he was a mere mortal, and as a way of dispersing any magic powers that he might possess.[15]

The three members of the entourage who escaped made it back to de Niza with the tragic news. What happened next is a mystery. Some believe that after raising a cross and claiming the region in the name of the viceroy, de Niza and his remaining party hastily retraced their steps to Mexico City, where his explanation to the viceroy of what happened at Cibola turned out to be completely false. In his report he gave dramatic details of Esteban's death (which he had not witnessed), and explained his own sacrificing and death-defying push to see Cibola for himself. He wrote:

---

15. There is a Zuni legend that tells of a "black Mexican with chili lips" who came from the "land of everlasting summer" and was killed by their ancestors.

"In the end, seeing that I was determined, two chiefs said that they would go with me [on to Hawikuh]. With these and my own Indian interpreters, I pursued my journey until I came within sight of Cibola, which is situated in a plain at the base of a round hill. It has the appearance of a very beautiful city, the best I have seen in these parts. The houses are of a style the Indians have described to me, all made of stone, with their stories and terraces, as it appeared to me from a hill where I was able to view it. The city is larger than the city of Mexico. At times I was tempted to go to it, because I knew I risked only my life, which had offered to God on the day I began this journey. But finally I realized, considering my danger, that if I died, I wouldn't be able to make my report of this country, which to me appears the greatest and best of the discoveries. I commented to the chiefs who had accompanied me; and they told me it was the poorest of the seven cities, and the Totonteac [thought to be one of the Hopi villages] is much larger and better than all the seven, and that it has so many houses and citizens it has no end. Under the circumstances, it seemed appropriate to me to call the country the new kingdom of Saint Francis; and there with the aid of the Indians, I made a great heap of stones, and on top of it placed a cross, small and light only because I had not the means of making it larger, and I declared that I erected that cross and monument in the name of Don Antonio de Mendoza, viceroy of New Spain, for the emperor, our Lord, as a sign of possession, conforming to my instruction, and by which possession I proclaim that I took all of the seven cities and the kingdoms of Totonteac and of Acus and of Marata, and that the reason I did not go to these latter places was in order to give an account of all I did and saw."

Researchers of New Spain's history have been baffled as to why de Niza wrote this inaccurate and absurd impression of his expedition: the mythical cities of gold, not to mention thousands of souls, were out there waiting to be redeemed. Alex Shoumatoff suggests that perhaps de Niza could not return empty-handed to the viceroy, or that the distinction between what was real and what was not wasn't always clear, particularly when one was traversing a desert awash with mirages.[16]

When Fray Marcos's story leaked out, all of Mexico City was abuzz. To keep the news from the ears of rival conquistadors in Cuba and Spain while he considered what to do, the viceroy banned everyone from leaving the colony without his permission. Clearly a full-scale military campaign was needed this time. It wasn't hard to find recruits for the expedition. The city was crawling with dashing young adventurers, eager for a

16. Ibid.

chance to venture forth into the great unknown to conquer vast new lands and treasure for Spain. To Francisco Vasquez de Coronado went the honor of leading the campaign. On February 22, 1540, he set out from Compostela, the capital of Nueva Galicia, leading an expedition of three hundred Spaniards, accompanied by hundreds of Indian allies, extra horses, and pack mules in search of the "Seven Cities." The entourage stretched for miles as it headed northward along the west coast of Mexico. Much of the journey was more difficult than expected, traversing miles of scorched and uninhabited desert.

Entering present-day Arizona a few miles west of Bisbee, they followed the San Pedro Valley and then headed eastward toward the Gila River, where they rested for several days. For another sixteen days, the convoy moved northward toward Cibola through the rugged White Mountains of eastern Arizona. An exhausted party finally reached Cibola (more likely Hawikuh) on July 7, 1540. It soon became obvious that de Niza's blooming metropolis had fallen far short of expectations. There were no roofs of gold. Pedro de Casteneda, the group's chronicler, describes what they saw: ". . . when they saw the first village, which was Cibola, such were the curses that some hurled at Friar Marcos that I pray God may protect him from them. It is a little, crowded village, looking as if it had been crumpled all up together."[17]

---

17. Marshall Trimble, *In Old Arizona* (1993).

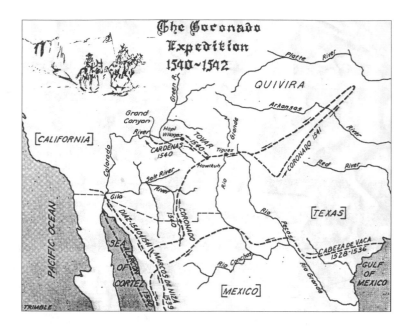

Map of the Coronado Expedition, 1590–1592.

Smoke signals on a nearby hill alerted the Spaniards that their arrival had not gone unnoticed. A clash ensued when Zuni leaders sent word to Coronado that his presence was not welcome. This fight of July 7, 1540 is considered the first formal engagement between the European invaders and the Indians in what is today the continental United States. Although a footnote in history, it nonetheless marks the beginning of the clash of two cultures that would be repeated many times over the next several hundred years.

Zuni warriors made a formidable stand, but Coronado's well-disciplined cavalry prevailed and the natives retreated to the sanctuary of their pueblos. Coronado then met with the Zuni headmen, exploring ways the two sides might co-exist peacefully. During the course of their meeting, the Zuni described seven villages some twenty-five leagues west where, on the high mesas, there lived the Tusayans. These people would later be called the Moquis by the Spaniards; today they are known as the Hopi.

Coronado sent out an exploratory party led by Pedro de Tovar to meet with them. As they drew near the village, the party was spotted by the villagers, who lined up for battle. The Hopitu had previously heard of the fierce bearded men soon after the Hawikuh battle. A skirmish ensued when Tovar, through an interpreter, demanded the village surrender and swear allegiance to the King of Spain. Peace was made when the headsmen appeared bearing gifts. It turned out that the Tusayans were waiting for a long-lost white brother whom they called Pahana.[18] At first they took de Tovar to be Pahana, but it soon became clear to them that de Tovar did not possess knowledge of their brotherhood symbol, and that he had forgotten the compact he had made with

---

18. Alex Shoumatoff, *Legends of the American Desert* (1997).

their grandfathers. In the parlays that followed, Tovar learned of a mighty river to the west.

Another expedition was hastily sent out led by Garcia Lopez de Cardenas to explore the possibility that this great river might very well be the fabled Strait of Anian, the mythical passage to the Orient. After several days of exploring the high plateau, they came upon the spectacular Grand Canyon, its immense vertical walls jutting up like medieval cathedrals. From where they stood on the rim, they saw the river snaking its way through the gorge far, far below. Tovar and his men spent the next few days poised on the verge, gazing upon this geological phenomenon, and examining ways to get to the bottom. Three soldiers tried to descend the almost vertical wall, but made it only part way before giving up.

When the discouraging news got back to Coronado, he decided against future quests to the west and turned his attention eastward toward the Rio Grande region. Coronado wrote a report to the viceroy on August 3, 1540 that condemned de Niza's report of the previous year as totally inaccurate: "the seven cities are seven small towns, all standing within four leagues of each other, and together they are called the kingdom of Cibola, which I have named Granada."

After two fruitless years searching for treasure, during which time extensive territories were claimed for Spain, Coronado and the remnants of his once impressive army returned to Mexico City in 1542.

This Bill Ahrendt painting depicts Garcia Lopez de Cardenas finding the Grand Canyon. (PHOTO: GARY M. JOHNSON)

Exhausted and believing that his efforts had been less than successful, he retired to his estate, never to reappear in the history of New Spain. He died in 1549. Dreams of finding cities of gold in the northern frontier lands were not being realized, as expedition after expedition found only the mud-walled villages of tribal people. Arizona was written off for the time being; New Mexico was seen as a more suitable area for colonization because of its river-roadway.

As the Spaniards pushed northward from Mexico City, it quickly became apparent they were entering a different cultural world from the Aztec-dominated one that they had first encountered in Mexico. The Indians to the northwest had built no empires comparable to those of the Aztecs and Tarascans. As they came to know these people, it became obvious that they constituted a cultural region of their own, delineated more or less on the east by the upper Rio Grande River, and on the north and west by the San Juan and Colorado Rivers. All but a small number were engaged in farming: growing beans, corn, and squash. The economy was simple whether agriculture was merely a supplement to gathering and hunting, or the primary basis of life. Each community was self-reliant. Trade extended widely throughout the region, but goods traded were rarely food or basic tools; they were luxury and ceremonial items such as paints, feathers, shells, and semiprecious stones. Rather than a regularized system of exchange of goods, trading was small-scale and infrequent.[19]

What the Spaniards came across in the northern fringes of their New World Empire was a region frozen in time since the collapse of the Hohokam and the Anasazi cultures. There were some forty-five tribal groups throughout an area stretching from Pueblo, New Mexico to the southern Sierra Madre—all of which lived in small, autonomous, and localized communities that were economically and politically independent of one another. They spoke twenty or more dissimilar languages with enough in common to show that they belonged to a single linguistic family. In these respects, the Indians presented a quite different set of problems to the Spaniards than did the Indians of central Mexico, where the existence of already developed dynasties made for easy conquest and cultural domination.

It took nearly two hundred years before Spanish exploration was able to determine the extent and intricacies of the inhabitants of the northern fringes. During this period, scores of exploratory expeditions and an expanded communication network across the region enabled the Spaniards to identify and distinguish the various groups and to give them distinct names.

By the early 1600s, the Spaniards were referring to a great majority of the natives of the northern fringes of New Spain as "rancheria" people, so named because

19. Edward H. Spicer, *Cycles of Conquest* (1997).

Map of Indian Tribes and Old Spanish Missions. (MAP: DEAN LYON; ART: JACK GRAHAM)

they lived in loose farming communities.[20] Within these *rancherias*, each family compound was situated within calling distance of the next. It is estimated that there were one hundred and fifty thousand Pimans, Yumans, Yaqui, and Opata of the "rancheria" group.

Then there were those whom the Spaniards called the "Village People." Fewer in number, they lived in multi-storied adobe complexes called pueblos. Included in this group were the Hopi on West Mesa in the barren rock desert of northeastern Arizona, as well as tribes that lived in the Rio Grande Valley. The Spaniards dubbed the third group "Band People." They were mostly Apaches who roamed in small groups on the fringes of Pueblo country, and who maintained a predatory relationship with the Village People, trading or raiding, depending on their circumstances.

---

20. Ibid.

4

PIMERIA ALTA

When Spanish ranchers and missionaries began
colonizing northern Sonora and southern Arizona
in the late 1600s, they called it Pimeria Alta.

Arizona's early history began in an area that extended
south from Tucson to the Mexican border. The
first missionaries came to the Santa Cruz Valley to
plant the seeds of Spanish culture. Following in their
footsteps were the soldiers and their families. The missionaries introduced new crops, animal husbandry,
and adobe construction. In return they expected the
natives to forsake time-honored customs and religion.
The Spanish explorers found neither the vast mineral
wealth that they so desperately sought in the 1500s,
nor a great river like the Rio Grande; if they had, the
history of the area might have been dramatically different. Fortunately, or unfortunately, depending on
one's point of view, neither happened. The Indian cultures north of the Gila River thus remained intact, and
those in southern Arizona (Pimeria Alta) stubbornly

retained much of their native culture. It wasn't until the late eighteenth century that Spain made a firm commitment to find a military solution to the Apache problem. Tucson, the "post farthest out," was to play a major role in this successful campaign.

Pimeria Alta, or Upper Pima country, came into focus at the end of the seventeenth century, when it first appeared on a 1696 map charted by the Jesuit missionary and explorer, Father Eusebio Francisco Kino. Autonomous groups of Piman-speaking O'odham inhabited an expansive desert region that extended from the Rio Concepcion-Rio Magdalena watershed on the south to the Gila and Salt Rivers on the north. The Spaniards called O'odham who cultivated irrigation farming along the rivers "Pimas"; they referred to those who lived in the arid western deserts as "Papagos." The O'odham themselves differentiate between the Ackimoel O'odham, or River People, and the Tohono O'odham, or Desert People. It was New Spain's northernmost district until the United States acquired it through the Gadsden Purchase Treaty in 1854. Nine years later, Pimeria Alta lost out to Arizona as the name chosen for the new territory carved out of western New Mexico.

The region, which Father Kino and his Jesuit brethren named Pimeria Alta, was occupied by as many as thirty thousand inhabitants. They were spread throughout an area extending from the Rio Concepcion-Rio Magdalena watershed to the Gila River, and from the San Pedro to the Colorado River. They lived

Father Eusebio Francisco Kino, Jesuit pathfinder and missionary to the Pimeria Alta.

Statue of Father Kino that stands in the Statuary Hall of the United States Congress.

in various kinds of village and transient communities scattered over an area immensely larger and far more difficult to traverse than the Opata country of central Sonora, where the Jesuits had been laboring for many years among the Opatas and the Lower Pimas. They were a single tribe only in the sense that they spoke dialects of a single language of Uto-Aztecan origin. There were marked cultural differences among them in the way that they lived, ranging from irrigation farming to nomadic gathering. Moreover, political organization of rancherias for any purpose other than warfare seemed to be unknown, although there were sports and customs of ceremonial cooperation between rancherias. The widest political organization probably did not link more than fifteen hundred people.

The Spaniards who came to know Pimeria Alta saw the Piman Indians as four major groups. In the southeastern part of what they called Pimeria Alta, bordering on the Opata-Eudeves of the upper San Miguel and upper Sonora Rivers, lived the people called Pimas (without the qualifying adjectives). To the west the Spaniards found that the Pimas made a distinction between themselves and the people who were said to be under the sway of a man named Soba; these people were called Sobas. Along the east and northeastern portion of Pimeria Alta resided people who seemed to the Spaniards to constitute a distinct group—the Sobaipuris. The fourth division of the Pimas remained somewhat vague as regards geographical extent, as well as population. These people gradually came to be called Papagos or Papabotas, a term used by the southern Pimas to refer vaguely to Piman-speakers to the north and northwest.

Father Kino and the Jesuits

The earliest written history of Pimeria Alta and its inhabitants revolves around the character of one man, Father Eusebio Francisco Kino, an energetic Italian Jesuit who was as much an explorer as missionary. In the spring of 1687, Father Kino began his missionary work among a group of Indians on the upper San Miguel River at the village of Cosari, where Pima and Opata tribal lands adjoined. At the time Father Kino began his work among the Upper Pimas, there was already a Spanish frontier settlement bordering on Piman lands—Bacanuche, which had been a flourishing mining town for thirty years. To the south in northern Mexico, missions had already been in operation among the Opata Indians as early as the 1630s, and had been flourishing in the Sonora River Valley since the 1640s.

Historian Edward H. Spicer writes that, when Kino set out to extend New Spain's northern frontier, there was considerable knowledge—both information and misinformation—of the Upper Pimas on the part of the Spaniards, and of the Spaniards on the part of some

Upper Pimas.[21] Just before Kino's arrival, a hostile encounter had resulted in a Piman leader from the vicinity of Huachuca being hanged by the Spaniards for conspiracy to carry out an uprising on the northwestern frontier. Two years later, in 1689, the Mututicachi rancheria, suspected of collaboration with hostile Indians, was attacked and destroyed by the Spaniards; all of its men were killed, and its women and children were deported to the south.

Kino's mission into the territory occurred at a time when financial support of the missionary program was considerably weaker than it had been at the beginning of the 1600s. Consequently, his work was slow in getting started. However, from his arrival in 1687 until his death in 1711, Father Kino labored vigorously among the scattered Piman rancheria people.

A missionary in New Spain enjoyed remarkable autonomy. From the beginning, popes recognized the immensity of the mission work and thus granted the missionary regulars the privileges of secular clergy. Persistently and with considerable success, the missionaries resisted intrusion into mission affairs and held on firmly to their sovereignty in spiritual, economic, and political matters. Their ideal was an absolute paternalism within the missions. The missionary had to provide for his Indians and discipline them with authority, otherwise he stood little chance of converting them.

21. Edward H. Spicer, *Cycles of Conquest* (1997).

Kino began his work among the Indians of Pimeria Alta at a time when mining and ranching had grown rapidly in central Sonora. The Opata Indians of the area were being absorbed into Spanish society as a result of these activities. As new mining opportunities were constantly opening up, there was a need for additional labor, and the most natural place to find it was among the Pimas, whom the Spaniards regarded as an extremely savage people. On the one hand, they were a threat to northward expansion; on the other, they were considered suitable only as laborers in the mines and on the ranches.

Aware of the extent of this attitude in the area and familiar with it elsewhere in New Spain, Father Kino made an effort before his assignment to the Pimeria Alta to get some special backing for the mission program that he proposed. In this regard, he secured from the viceroy in Mexico City a special *credula* that affirmed the declared policy of no forced labor and the exemption of Indians from tribute during the missionary program. The governor of Sonora reluctantly accepted the program, but antagonism to the missionary program was expressed in rumors and surreptitious gossip against the Pimas and the mission work among them. The charges were that Pimas cooperated with the Jocomes and Apaches in the escalating border fighting to the east, and that they were a generally wild and difficult people. Kino set out from the start to gather evidence against these charges and demonstrated quickly that, with rare exception, the Pimas were peaceful and quite ready to ally themselves directly with the Spaniards against the Jocome-Apache raiders, or to live quietly under the mission system.

Kino worked single-handedly for some five years as the only missionary among the Upper Pimas, but received some essential support from military and civil authorities. Most notable in this regard was Captain Juan Mateo Manje, who accompanied the priest on his early trips of exploration. Kino established a mission at Dolores that would become his headquarters during the subsequent twenty-four years he worked among the Pimas. He had two able helpers with whom he worked closely during the early years. The first was an interpreter named Francisco Cantor, who was also a trained catechist. Said to have had wide influence among the Pimas of the upper San Miguel and Magdalena River Valleys, Coxi was the second and accompanied Kino to the various rancherias that he wished to visit.

Kino's method of administering to the Natives was not to establish himself at a single mission site and limit himself to one small specific area; instead he employed an extended method, that of an itinerant preacher visiting rancherias, meeting the natives, and designating certain rancherias as mission sites. By the end of 1689, he had established contacts with the Pimas on the upper Altar at El Tupo, Tubutama, Saric, and Tucubavia. Next, he began visits to the relatively heavy Pima population of the upper Santa Cruz River at Tumacacori and Guevavi. At these places, he gave out food, spoke about the Christian faith, baptized a few children, and talked with the chiefs about the mission program.

Acculturation was a gradual process. By 1693, much of present-day Sonora was under the mission system. Cattle herds and tillage were flourishing at Dolores, Cocospera, San Ignacio, and Tubutama. In 1694, Spanish soldiers joined with Opatas in repelling a Jocome-Apache raid on the Opata mission at Cuchuta, a few miles south of the Fronteras presidio. It appeared to Kino that his work among the Pimas was paying dividends. They were steadily accepting the missions; converts were being made by the hundreds; and they were allying themselves with the Spaniards against the increasing threat of raids from the northeast.

However, the peaceful course of events in Pimeria Alta was upset in 1695, when the pressure of conquest from the south upset the balance of Indian relations in several northern frontier areas. Northwest Sonora was increasingly feeling the consequences of Indian reaction to conquest, particularly the Spanish ranchers in northern Sonora who were suffering the loss of livestock and occasional deaths from Indian raids. The Spaniards were not sure which Indians were implicated, and many residents of the border towns implicated the Pima.

Ruins of Kino Mission at Cocospera, just below the Arizona-Mexico border. The original mission was established in 1689. (PHOTO: MARSHALL TRIMBLE)

Feelings against Opatas came to a head in 1695, when the peaceful Pimas of Tubutama killed the mission's Opata overseer and two assistants. They next destroyed Altar and, entering Caborca, murdered a young missionary who had recently arrived at his post. As it turned out, they were a group of dissidents and not representative of the mission pueblo. Spanish reprisal was swift. General Jironza and a contingent of soldiers marched into Pima country and, upon finding few Pimas to take action against, killed some women and boys. They destroyed crops at Caborca, as a lesson to the Indians, and then decided that since there was no general uprising it would be best to work out a peaceful settlement.

Father Kino persuaded the Pima leaders who had not taken part in the killings to bring together their people and the leaders of the rebellious group with the Spaniards at El Tupo. The meeting was arranged and the headman of El Tupo proceeded to point out the men responsible for the killing. As soon as the first guilty man was pointed out, one of the Spanish officers in the arena drew his sword and beheaded him. Then the Spaniards and their Seri allies went berserk, killing more than fifty Pimas in a matter of minutes, including the peaceful headman of El Tupo and the leaders to whom Kino had promised immunity. Most of the slaughtered were innocent bystanders, victims of what might be seen as a breakdown of military discipline. The result was an outbreak of war.

Pima forces organized and destroyed Tubutama and Caborca. Heading east they moved on Imuris and San Ignacio and destroyed the churches there. Spanish forces numbering three hundred moved through Pima country and, when they were unable to flush out the Piman attackers, turned to killing women and children. The Spaniards offered to negotiate once more and again Kino took the lead in finding peaceful headmen at Caborca, Tucubavia, and El Tupo who would negotiate. The Pimas, recognizing that they were no contest for the Spanish military, turned over those who had engineered the killing of the Opatas and thereafter relations improved.

In the aftermath of the uprising, much work had to be done to redevelop the devastated area, as well as to build renewed trust and relationships with the Indians. Somehow, Father Kino's reputation as an honest and trustworthy individual survived among the Indians, and the military believed that Kino was the best insurance they had against more Indian uprisings.

In 1696, while the mission program in the devastated area was being redeveloped, Kino undertook missionary work to the Sobaipuris in the northeast. In March 1699, he and Juan Mateo Manje, the second-highest civil official in Sonora, explored Tohono O'odham (Papago) country as far west as the Colorado. They visited the Sobaipuri Pimas along the Santa Cruz and San Pedro Rivers, and traveled as far north as the Salt River Valley, where Kino preached to the Gilenos, as the Ackimuel O'odham living along the Salt and Gila Rivers were called.

It has been said that wherever Kino went, the O'odhams welcomed him, responding warmly to his personality and charisma. They also appreciated the material gifts that he distributed to them: grain seeds, fruit trees, and small herds of livestock. These goodwill gestures were employed by the missionaries in their policy of *reduccion*—the clustering of Indians in villages where they could be more easily catechized

Mission of San Jose de Tumacacari.

Mission San Jose de Tumacacori c. 1864. First visited by Father Kino in 1691, it did not become a full-fledged mission until 1771. (SKETCH: J. ROSS BROWNE)

and controlled. While Kino had much success in clustering the O'odham to the south, he was less fortunate with the Ackimoel O'odham who resisted all Christianization efforts.

In Pimeria Alta, the mission program proceeded slowly. Kino founded the missions of San Xavier and San Miguel at the Piman communities of Bac and Guevavi along the Santa Cruz; but the Jesuits soon abandoned these northern outposts, and they were not re-staffed until 1732, twenty-one years after Kino died.

The rest of Pimeria Alta never came under Spanish control. Nonetheless, both the Sobaipuris along the San Pedro River and the Gilenos along the Gila became staunch allies of the Spaniards, fighting the Apaches and serving as a listening post during both the Spanish and Mexican periods.[22] It has been said that without the O'odham allies, Hispanic Arizona would not have survived.

The Sobaipuris never got the resident missionary that they had so often requested, and the presidio built at Terrenate, on the upper San Pedro River, offered little protection to their settlements. In due course, they moved out of the area. In 1732 some Sobaipuris, under their leader Humari, left to merge with the Sobaipuris of the Gila River to the northwest; the few who remained left in 1762 to join the people in Suamca, Bac, and Tucson. The populous upper Santa Cruz and Bac areas were still without regular visiting missionaries. The Papago country to the west, although rather well explored by Kino, remained undeveloped. Indians who had gathered at Bac, Suamca, and Quiburi in the 1720s, in expectation of the coming missionaries, began to disperse.[23]

The Spanish settlers were by no means pleased with the missionary program. Increasingly, they felt that it conflicted with their interests. In the early 1700s,

22. Keiran McCarty, *Desert Documentary* (1976).
23. Edward H. Spicer, *Cycles of Conquest* (1997).

miners and settlers supported a proposal that mission lands be distributed among the Indians, that the missions be secularized, and that Indians be rounded up for work in the mines and on the ranches. The twenty-year exemption of Indians from paying tribute and *repartimiento*, which Kino had worked out with the viceroy, had expired. Settlers saw it as an opportunity to petition the removal of the Jesuits and to do away with the mission program. This discontent with missionary activities coincided with a twenty-five year decline in the Pimeria. By 1730 there had been no increase in the number of missions over those established by Kino.

In 1732 missionary activity again shifted to the northern area. Three new missionaries were assigned to work on the upper and middle Santa Cruz River—at Suamca, Guevavi, and Bac—and the O'odham again started to gather around those missions. Father Joseph de Torres Perea's account of conditions at Bac in 1744 sheds some light on what mission operations must have been like at the time. He wrote:

"The Mission which is ministered to simultaneously with that of Guebavi in Pimeria Alta, is 25 leagues distant from Guebavi toward the North over a road scant in water and dangerous because of the enemy. Toward the North there no longer are Christians, but various gentile nations without the light of the Gospel nor knowledge of Christ. This

Mission was founded the same year as Guebavi, that is 1732, and since then until the present year 1744 shows on its baptismal register 2,142 without counting those whom other Fathers baptized before, in whose books I think they were recorded.

"It is a well-populated Mission. There were more than 400 families. It is a mission of Indians who are still mountain-dwellers, little or not all amenable to the subjection of the gentle yoke of Christ. They are Christians more in name than reality. Only two Missionary Fathers lived in this Mission. They bewitched one in the year 1732; they rose up and profaned the vestments and chalices. Afterwards they surrendered, and now live quietly. Since then they have been ministered to by those who are Missionaries of Guebavi (because of the scarcity of Missionaries) who cannot do what is necessary fully to teach and minister to them, because of the distance and risky terrain.

"These Indians still appear to live like gentiles with the difference that in their paganism they were not baptized as they now are, without any change in their way of life. They know not how to pray, not even the 'Our Father' nor the 'Hail, Mary,' nor to cross themselves. Many adults flee from baptism, and I have found old and very old gentiles. The majority, and nearly all, marry according to their pagan rite: they really work at avoiding being married by the Church. In this matter they hide the truth from the Missionary Fathers, telling them that they had been married by the Church by previous Fathers. This is not true, because I convince them with the marriage registers in which one does not find thirty couples married by the church, there being more than 400 families. Yet they are not convinced. The poor Fathers work hard in this, but because the jurisdiction is large, it is not remedied according to one's wishes. Dated in Pimeria Alta on the sixteenth day of March of 1744. Joseph de Torres Perea."[24]

By 1750 there were nine Jesuit missionaries among the Upper Pimas, and work was again proceeding as smoothly and as confidently as it had in the early days in the Pimeria. The Jesuits were even considering plans to extend their missionary work far into the north country, in response to an appeal from the Hopis who were refusing to cooperate with the Franciscans of New Mexico. Inadequate support from the military, which lacked the resources and the desire to push the frontier further north, as well as a change of heart by the Hopi, impeded further expansion of the missions. Hispanic Arizona, which never amounted to more than a thousand non-Indian people clinging to settlements

---

24. Henry F. Dobyns, *Spanish Colonial Tucson* (1961). (Translated by Dobyns from the original document Number 48 in its Mexican Manuscript collection, housed at the Bancroft Library, University of California, Berkeley).

like Tubac and Tucson in the Santa Cruz Valley, continued for the most part as a vast alien *terra firma* of unexplored mountains and deserts.

Another uprising of the O'odham occurred in 1751 under the leadership of Luis Oacpicagigua, who rebelled against the harsh discipline of several Jesuit missionaries. However, most believe he wanted to be chief of all the Pimas, with the objective of ousting the Spaniards from Pima territory. Luis and his followers killed two padres and more than a hundred Spanish settlers before the revolt diffused. Luis surrendered to the Spaniards at Tubac on the Santa Cruz River, and the uprising ended in a negotiated settlement with the O'odham rebels that restored the status quo in return for the removal of the most obnoxious priests. It was not a widespread movement, but the ambitions of one man who stirred up trouble in the belief that he could muster enough support from among the Pimas for his personal cause.

The 1751 Pima revolt constituted a shock from which the Jesuit missions failed to recover by the time of their expulsion sixteen years later. To prevent further uprisings among the O'odham and to provide protection for the Bac and Guevavi Missions, a new presidio (garrison) was established at Tubac—the first Spanish military outpost in what is present-day Arizona.

In a climate of reform following the inauguration of Charles III of Spain, the Jesuits were expelled from throughout the Spanish Empire, including northwestern

New Spain. For nearly seventy-five years, they had preached to the Natives and isolated them into autonomous mission communities to shield them from the perceived corrupt ways of the soldiers and settlers. In areas where they were successful, they also dominated Indian land and labor. As Spanish ranchers and miners settled along the mission frontier, bitter competition for Indian resources broke out between the missionaries and the colonists.

The captain of the Tubac Presidio was one Juan Bautista de Anza, who was appointed to the post in 1760. He wrote in a personal-service report in 1767: "When I took over my present command in 1760, my section of the frontier was faced with an uprising of over a thousand Papagos. After launching various campaigns to subjugate them, I attacked them personally on May 10, 1760, and took the lives of Ciprian, their captain, and nine others. During the same year of 1760, I was sent down to the Seri frontier five times and led three campaigns. I killed thirty in 1762 and captured many members of their families . . . "[25]

By the 1760s, it had become clear that the northern defenses were not functioning as they should. A royal commission was dispatched from Mexico City to recommend how the presidios might be realigned. The survey, which took two years, advised numerous changes and

---

25. Keiran McCarty, *Desert Documentary* (1976). (Translated from the original on folio 263 of volume 47 of the Provincias Internas section of the Archivo General de la Nacion in Mexico City).

the relocation of several presidios. In the summer of 1771, a council sitting in Mexico City approved the findings of the report and forwarded it to Madrid. Its recommendations resulted in the *Reglamento* of 1772—a major reorganization of the presidial system.

The Jesuits won many skirmishes with colonial officials, but in 1767 they lost the war.[26] On the holiday of Saint John the Baptist (June 24, 1767), German-born Jesuit Father Joseph Och and his fellow-Jesuits were having a cool drink after a hectic holiday in the cloister garden of the Colegio Maximo de San Pedro y San Pablo, the order's principal house in Mexico City. At three in the afternoon, a captain whom they knew strode into the garden. Silently hundreds of soldiers had taken up position in the streets. A commotion in the hall outside his room aroused Father Och. The military had cut the bell ropes so that no alarm could be rung. All the Jesuits, some only half dressed, were being herded into the chapel. Later, the king's minister extraordinary to New Spain, Jose de Galvez, entered the chapel with the father superior. After a role call, all the Jesuits were ordered to surrender their keys. When they had done so, "a quivering and weeping secretary" read the tersely worded royal decree: "Because of weighty considerations which his majesty keeps hidden in his heart, the entire Society of Jesus and all Jesuits must leave the country, and their

26. Thomas E. Sheridan, *Arizona, A History* (1995).

establishments and properties must be turned over to the Royal treasurer."[27]

Twelve hundred miles north of Mexico City, late in July of the same year, a detachment of soldiers from the Altar Presidio rode unannounced into the mission pueblo of Guevavai. The army ordered Father Custodio Ximeno to turn over his keys, and instructed him not to speak to anyone, least of all to the bewildered Pimas. While the soldiers locked up the church valuables and made arrangements for food rations for the Indians, Father Ximeno hurriedly packed a few meager belongings. Then the soldiers mounted their horses and led him away. At Tubac, the commanding officer, Captain Juan Bautista de Anza, accepted his part in the expulsion stoically, saying "that after all, the King commands it and there may be more to it than we realize. The thoughts of men differ as much as the distance from earth to heaven."

Franciscans Replace the Jesuits

The crown's reform-minded aides would have preferred to secularize all ex-Jesuit missions immediately, believing that it was time for the long-dependent mission Indians to be transformed into productive, taxpaying subjects. But few secular priests wanted, or were

---

27. John Kessel, *Friars, Soldiers and Reformers: Hispanic Arizona and the Sonora Mission Frontier 1767–1856* (1976).

available, to take over where the Jesuits had left off. Instead, the Franciscan friars agreed to accept the charge of the northwest missions, and there was a slow rebirth of the missionary program. The reformers moved to throw out the traditional paternalism along with the Jesuits, thus granting the Indians a degree of civil rights and putting mission financial affairs into the hands of government agents. The Franciscans protested vehemently; they begged that the old system be maintained, pointing to the success of their fellow Franciscans in Texas rather than to that of the discredited Jesuits. Faced with the rapidly worsening conditions of the missions, the reformers yielded.

The thirty-year-old Spaniard Father Francisco Garcés, ordained a priest in the Franciscan order just four years earlier, arrived as the new missionary at San Xavier, the northernmost mission protected by the Tubac Presidio. Father Francisco Garcés was at San Xavier less than one year, when he sent a documented report to Governor Pineda that detailed accounts of the attacking Apaches and the defenseless Pimas of the Tucson area. He petitioned for a presidio at Tucson. From the date that he arrived in 1768 until his death at Yuma in 1781, he became one of the great missionaries in the history of the Spanish borderlands.

In the latter half of the eighteenth century, Captain Juan Bautista de Anza and Father Francisco Garcés sought to extend the Spanish frontier deeper into what is now the state of Arizona. Much has been written

Dedication of a monument in honor of Father Francisco Garcés at Yuma.

about the new beginning made by this pairing of a frontier captain and a frontier missionary nearly a century after the pioneering efforts of Eusebio Francisco Kino. However, in emphasizing their epic expeditions westward to establish an overland route to California, their equally important activities at home have been neglected.

Hopes of northward expansion continued to kindle in the minds of the dauntless Spaniards; and, in 1775, Juan Bautista de Anza led a group of Spanish colonists

Lieutenant Colonel Juan Bautista de Anza, commandant of the Presidio de Tubac, crossing the Colorado River in 1775. (PAINTING: THERESA POTTER)

from Tubac to San Francisco Bay. Five years later, the Spaniards tried to secure this route by establishing a settlement at Yuma, along the Colorado. But the Yuman-speaking Quechan Indians—veterans of countless encounters against their Cocopa, Maricopa and O'odham enemies—revolted. On the morning of July 17, 1781, they surprised the Spaniards during mass and slaughtered them, including Father Garcés. The Yuma revolt turned California into an "island" and Arizona into a "cul de sac," severing the Arizona-California connection before it could be firmly fixed.[28] It left Arizona exposed and besieged.

The region was both a homeland and a sanctuary for the predatory Apaches, to whom livestock raiding was a traditional livelihood. The settlement in the Santa Cruz Valley threatened to break under the strain of Apache hostility, and harassed settlers living along the fertile banks of the Santa Cruz River fled their homes. "Hispanic Arizona" was reduced to the failing mission pueblo of Guevavi; three vistas: Calabazas, Sonoita, and Tumacacori, the fifty-man garrison at Tubac; and San Savier del Bac with its Tucson vista.

Father Ximeno, in charge of Guevavi, wanted to abandon the mission and move to more populous Tumacacori, fifteen miles north and close to Tubac. But his superiors would not consent to it. Instead, when a replacement for San Xavier failed to emerge,

---

28. David Weber, *The Spanish Frontier in North America* (1992).

Ximeno found himself in charge of missionary activity in the entire valley from Guevavi to Tucson. In 1797, an expedition by Jose de Zuniga, captain of the Tucson Presidio, chartered a route between Tucson and the Zuni Pueblos. But Apache hostilities prevented that route from coming into frequent use, and so Pimeria Alta remained an isolated peninsula in a sea of hostility.

When they arrived in Pimeria Alta, the Franciscans found the eighty-year-old Jesuit foundations crumbling. They endured for seventy-five more years under the most adverse conditions. They used the same methods as their predecessors, and they fought just as hard to maintain their autonomy. The Jesuits came from all parts of Europe, the Franciscans from Spain or Spanish America.

5

THE PUEBLO OF
SAN AGUSTIN DE TUSCON

"I selected and marked out in the presence of
Father Francisco Garcés and Lieutenant Juan de
Carmona a place known as San Agustin del
Tucson as the new site of the presidio . . . on
this Twentieth Day of August of the year 1775."
—Don Hugo O'Conor

Major changes to New Spain's northern presidial
system, endorsed in Marques de Rubi's *Reglamento* of 1772, were carried out by an Irishman named
Don Hugo O'Conor. The Indians called him "Capitan
Colorado" because of his ruddy face and red hair. Born
in Ireland in 1734, Hugo was one of the "Wild Geese"
who had fled English-occupied Ireland to fight in the
service of the King of Spain. At thirty-one years old, he
was already a major and Knight of the Order of Cala-
trava when he reached Mexico City in 1765, as part
of a commission to reorganize the army of New Spain.
Dissatisfied with his staff job, he managed to secure a
presidial command on the frontier. By 1774, O'Conor,

now a full colonel, was placed in charge of the entire frontier as Commandant Inspector, with instructions to put in place de Rubi's proposals. For the next six years, O'Conor traveled some 12,000 miles on horseback, inspecting and realigning the frontier presidios. Upon finishing his mission in 1778, he was promoted to Brigadier-General and appointed Governor and Captain General of the Province of Yucatan. He died the following year.

The presidial realignments were only part of much broader reforms decreed by Spain's Bourbon king, Carlos III. In 1776, he decreed that the border provinces of New Spain be removed from the jurisdiction of the viceroy in Mexico City. He instead placed them directly under the Spanish Crown through a newly-created office that consolidated civil and military powers. This office possessed the authority to take decisive action, as necessary, against Indian and European rivals. Spanish officials saw expansion by the Russians down the Pacific Coast and by the British in the Mississippi Valley as a threat to their interests in the region, particularly regarding the rich silver-mining areas of Zacatecas and San Luis Potosf.

As part of the realignment scheme for Pimeria Alta, O'Conor planned the relocation of several presidios in 1775: Santa Cruz Presidio relocated north to the west bank of the San Pedro River, near a former Sobaipuri village; Fronteras moved to San Bernardino; and Tubac shifted to Tucson. Established in 1752, Tubac was providing ample protection for the missions at Tumaca-cori and Guevavi; but for San Xavior del Bac and the other settlements on the lower Santa Cruz, a cry for help might take as long as two days to answer. Because the military had decided it could not afford two pre-sidios in the region, the solution, as O'Conor envi-sioned it, was to move the presidio out of Tubac and place it at the more strategic San Cosme de Tucson.

At O'Conor's side when he announced his decision was Father Francisco Thomas Garcés of San Xavior del Bac. For him O'Conor's decision was the accumulation of seven years of work, politics, and prayer. Father Garcés had come to take charge of the little mission of San Xavior del Bac seven years earlier, when the Fran-ciscans replaced the Jesuits who were expelled from the Spanish Empire. The Franciscans renamed Tucson San Augustine, but its status remained that of a visita attached to the San Xavicr dcl Bac Mission. For Fathcr Gracés and the gray-robed Franciscans at Bac and else-where, mission work on the frontier lacked the influ-ence and prestige that their black-robed predecessors had enjoyed. In fact, Spanish reformers toyed with the idea of abolishing the missions once and for all, but abandoned that scheme as soon as they realized that the missions were the cheapest and the most effective way to control Christianized Indians.

The winds of social and economic change were fan-ning a new era. To quote historian Thomas E. Sheridan, ". . . a new order had arisen in northern New Spain, one that reflected a fundamental change of European society and the colonies Europe controlled. The world economy was growing more and more capitalistic as medieval privileges crumbled. Consequently, resources such as land and labor became commodities in the marketplace rather than rights and duties locked up in a feudal order. The Jesuit dream of independent missions contradicted the entrepreneurial dream of abundant land and a mobile labor force. With the Jesuits gone and the Franciscans weakened, it became much easier for Spanish settlers to exploit that land and labor for private use."

Early on the morning of August 20, 1775, while the air was still chilly, a party—Father Garcés, O'Conor, his aide, and a handful of Indians—rode north from San Xavier del Bac Mission along the river toward Tucson. They passed by irrigated fields where beans, maize, squash, melons, and wheat grew in abundance. As they rode, O'Conor observed the richness of the land and the relatively substantial supply of water and pasturage it produced. As he rode on, his military-trained eye surveyed the landscape with satisfaction at its strategic value. After an hour or two spent surveying the crudely barricaded site, the party mounted their horses and headed back to the mission at Bac.

That evening, O'Conor wrote out the order that established Tucson:

"I selected and marked out in the presence of Father Francisco Garcés and Lieutenant Juan de

Carmona a place known as San Agustin del Tucson as the new site of the presidio (now located at San Ignacio de Tubac). It is situated at a distance of eighteen leagues from Tubac, fulfills the requirements of water, pasture and wood, and effectively closes the Apache frontier. The designation of the new presidio becomes official with the signatures of myself, Father Francisco Garcés and Lieutenant Juan de Carmona, at this mission of San Xavier del Bac, on this Twentieth Day of August of the year 1775."[29]

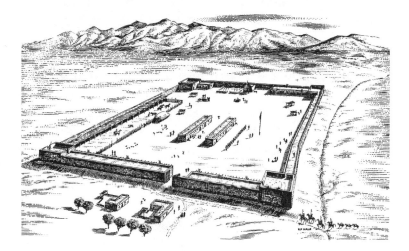

Artist Cal Peter's conception of the Royal Spanish Presidio at Tuscon c. 1795.

---

29. John Bret Harte, *Tucson Portrait of a Desert Pueblo* (1980).

The three men signed it. However, it was one thing to decree the establishment of a presidio, but quite another to establish it. Captain Juan Bautista de Anza, the Tubac commander, was not present at the signing. He was on an expedition to found the city of San Francisco, and afterwards to Mexico City in preparation for his appointment as military governor of Sonora. Because of his absence, no action was undertaken to implement the move until 1776; his deputy at Tubac, Lieutenant Juan de Oliva, was in no hurry to move. He had been attached to the Tubac Garrison since its founding twenty-three years earlier.

While the troops assigned to defend the mission and settlement remained inaccessible forty miles to the south, however, Apache raids continued around Bac and Tucson. Finally in early 1776, Lt. Juan Marie de Oliva led a small party of troops to Tucson to begin construction of the new presidio. As de Anza had taken most of the troops to California, Oliva was left shorthanded, delaying for the time being much of the construction work on the fort.

In 1777, the Tubac community wrote to their former commander, now the military governor of Sonora, complaining that Apache raids on Tubac had increased by the day since the garrison was moved to Tucson. They described how the Apaches had stolen their horses and cattle, destroyed their fields, and carried off what corn they could. They referred to the untold casualties that the Tubac settlement and the surrounding

Pima villages had suffered since the move, and to the total destruction of Calabazas by fire. They appealed for the restoration of the presidio to its original location and for the positioning of troops along the Apache attack and escape routes.

De Anza reviewed the plight of his old command and even considered recommending that the presidio be moved back to Tubac. But the presidio was not returned to the frightened citizens of Tubac. The best that de Anza could do was to assign a dozen or so men to protect Tubac and the missions of Tumacacori and Calabazas. Captain Don Pedro de Allande arrived in early 1777 to take charge of the Tucson Garrison. The new commandant, appalled at the lack of combat readiness he found, ordered a speedup on construction. Though still in his mid-thirties, he was a seasoned veteran of several European engagements.

In its early years, the Tucson Garrison was not able to deter the Apaches from raiding. In November 1779, a force of Apaches estimated at 350 attacked the presidio. After a long and intense battle, the Apaches withdrew. Among the Indian casualties was a chief whose head Captain de Allande severed and mounted on a lance atop the stockade. Tucson's severest attack occurred on May Day 1782, when as many as six hundred Apaches stormed the presidio, bent on taking the fort. In the fierce fighting that followed, Captain de Allande was severely wounded, but his well-disciplined troops prevailed in holding off the Apache. In

April 1783 and again in January 1785, Pima troops of the San Rafael Company, hot on the Apaches' trail, ran into disastrous ambushes sprung by the enemy.

The Apache menace did not lessen. The ghastly sun-shriveled Apache heads staring from atop the Tucson Presidio stockade wall testified to the continuing hostilities. Captain de Allande displayed the grisly trophies "in honor of the military might of his majesty . . . causing terror among the barbarians . . ." Apache attacks continued to beset the community through much of the 1780s. Tucson was not merely the farthest outpost on the Sonoran frontier; it was also a critical link in land communication with California.

Captain de Allande had led several successful campaigns into Apacheria before his transfer in 1786. His search and destroy missions proved to be a formidable strategy in defeating the nomadic warriors on their own turf. The Spaniards did not rely solely on military action to combat the Apaches. In the late 1780s, Viceroy Bernard de Galvez instituted an insidious scheme of chicanery. He ordered his military commanders to offer those Apaches who agreed to stop fighting free provisions: "defective firearms, strong liquor, and such other commodities as would render them militarily and economically dependent on the Spaniards."[30] This scheme, known as the Galvez Plan, was remarkably successful in bringing about peace with the Apaches, and

---

30. Thomas E. Sheridan, *A History of the Southwest* (1995).

the so-called "golden years" followed. Hispanic Arizona prospered moderately during the last years of Spanish rule. Mines were opened; land grant ranches increased; and the beautiful mission churches of San Xavier del Bac and San Jose de Tumacacori were constructed.[31]

The total non-Indian population, as pointed out by anthropologist James Officer, never amounted to more than a thousand individuals stubbornly clinging to settlements like Tucson and Tubac. Whenever Hispanic ranchers, farmers, and miners tried to expand into the San Pedro Valley or into the grasslands of southeastern Arizona, the Apaches drove them back. For most of the residents of Tucson and the surrounding neighborhood, their economy was never much beyond the subsistence level. As Captain Jose de Zuniga noted in his official report to the Royal Board of Trade in 1804, "The only public work here that is truly worthy of this report is the church at San Xavier del Bac."[32] Built by the O'odham, under the direction of Franciscans between 1779 and 1797, Bac was a baroque glory. Zuniga dismissed the other missions along the Santa Cruz as mere chapels.

The rest of southern Arizona remained in Native American hands: Tohono O'odham in the western deserts; Pimas in the San Pedro Valley; Apaches in the eastern mountain ranges; and Yumans along the Colorado River. The Apache *mansos*—the tame ones who

31. Marshall Trimble, *In Old Arizona* (1993).
32. James E. Officer, *Arizona, 1536–1856* (1987).

lined up outside the walls at Tucson and several other presidios for their weekly handout of maize, meat, and tobacco—became a source of contention between the friars and the presidio captains. The padres maintained that not enough attention was being given to the Indians' spiritual welfare. As a solution, the friars suggested subjecting these Apaches to a mission-like environment, but the authorities ignored them.

The Mexican Revolution had little effect on Tucson. Life remained simple for the self-reliant frontier people. The subsistence-farmers had limited commerce or contact with the outside world. In the 1830s, the Apaches resumed warfare. Officials of the new Mexican Republic were too busy with other matters in the capital to worry about frontier settlements. The amenities offered the Apaches under the Galvez Plan were discontinued, leaving the brave natives of Tucson to fend for themselves.

With the exception of a few "mountain men" who entered Arizona in the early 1820s, few Anglo-Americans had set foot in the old pueblo. The first recorded visit was on May 31, 1826, when three unidentified Anglo-Americans showed up at the presidio. Their visit is believed to mark the beginning of Anglo-American infiltration into Hispanic Arizona. From 1826 on, a drifting array of trappers, traders, and bounty hunters wandered in and out of the Santa Cruz Valley. One California-bound party of eleven trappers led by a David Jackson stopped at Tucson in October 1831. The only comment recorded by the group was by a Jonathan Warner, who referred to the place briefly as "a military post and small town."[33]

Tucson was still a sleepy village on December 17, 1846, when a Mormon battalion stopped off to replenish supplies on its way to California. Battalion commander Captain Phillip St. George Cooke was rebuffed when he sent warm greetings to the presidio commandant. At any rate, Cooke's battalion entered the pueblo while Commandant Antonio Comaduran discreetly withdrew his troops and a number of citizens to San Xavier. He moved them nine miles to the south, rather than have any contact with the Americans.

Thirty years later on March 10, 1856, the United States flag was raised over Tucson. For Captain Hilaron Garcia, it was anything but an ordinary day as *Pueblo* captain. Several days earlier, he had received orders to vacate the Tucson Garrison of its small contingent of Mexican troops, and the historic day had arrived to move out. In military fashion, Garcia lowered the Mexican flag from the flagpole, assembled his soldiers and their families, and began a leisurely march down the road toward Sonora.

At that historic moment, a small group of Americans led by Bill Kirkland hoisted the Stars and Stripes atop the roof of Miles Mercantile Store. Tucson was now officially part of the United States. John Butterfield's

33. Marshall Trimble, *Roadside History of Arizona* (1986).

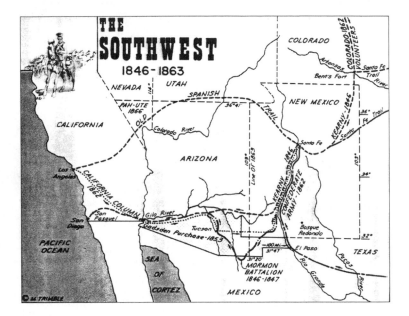

Map of the Southwest, 1846–1863. (MAP: DEAN LYON; ART: JACK GRAHAM)

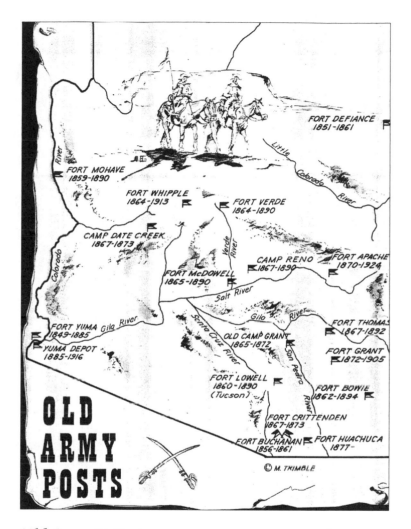

FORT DEFIANCE
1851-1861

FORT MOHAVE
1859-1890

FORT WHIPPLE
1864-1913

FORT VERDE
1864-1890

CAMP DATE CREEK
1867-1873

CAMP RENO
1867-1890

FORT APACHE
1870-1924

FORT McDOWELL
1865-1890

FORT YUMA
1849-1885

YUMA DEPOT
1885-1916

OLD CAMP GRANT
1865-1872

FORT THOMAS
1867-1892

FORT GRANT
1872-1905

FORT LOWELL
1860-1890
(Tucson)

FORT BOWIE
1862-1894

FORT CRITTENDEN
1867-1873

FORT BUCHANAN
1856-1861

FORT HUACHUCA
1877-

© M. TRIMBLE

OLD ARMY POSTS

Old Army Posts. (MAP: DEAN LYON; ART: JACK GRAHAM)

famous leather-slung stagecoaches rumbled into town in 1858, linking Tucson with the rest of the country. By 1860 Tucson's six hundred and fifty residents made up the bulk of Arizona's non-Indian population.

The withdrawal of federal troops following the outbreak of the Civil War made Tucson one of the few sanctuaries in the territory. Ranchers, miners, and settlers—all fleeing the ferocious Apache attacks—gathered inside the adobe periphery of the old pueblo to await the army's return. Relief came when Captain Sherod Hunter and fifty-four mounted riflemen arrived on February 28, 1862. It mattered little that the uniforms they wore were chestnut and gray, and that the flag they hoisted was that of the Confederacy; besieged Tucsonians were happy to have a military shield once again. But the Confederate occupation of Tucson was brief. Three months later, a regiment of California Volunteers arrived to hoist the Stars and Stripes once more.

According to contemporary sources, Tucson was a favorite gathering place for scoundrels of all sorts throughout the latter part of the nineteenth century. Crime was rampant. As first mentioned by Captain John C. Cremony, "Innocent and unoffending men were shot down or bowie-knifed merely for the pleasure of witnessing their death agonies. Men walked the streets and public squares with double-barreled shotguns and hunted each other as sportsmen hunt for game. In the graveyard of Tucson there were forty-seven graves of white men in 1860, ten years after the events above recited, and of that number only two had died natural deaths, all the rest being murdered in brawls and barroom quarrels." [34]

When John G. Bourke visited Tucson as a young lieutenant in 1869, he wrote of the place as follows:

"My eyes and ears were open to the strange scenes and sounds which met them on every side. Tucson was a foreign town as if it were in Hayti instead of within our own borders. The language, dress, funeral processions, religious ceremonies, feasts, dances, games, joys, perils, griefs, and tribulations of its populations were something not to be looked for in the region east of the Missouri river. . . . Each heart is gay for we have at last reached Tucson, the commercial *entrepot* of Arizona and the remoter southwest—Tucson, the Mecca of the dragoon, the Naples of the desert, which one was to see and die; Tucson whose alkali pits yielded water sweeter than the Well of Zemzen, whose maidens were more charming, whose society was more hospitable, merchants more progressive, magazines better stocked, climate more dreamy, than any other town from Santa Fe to Los Angeles. . . ."[35]

The Tucson that the critically astute Bourke visited in 1869 was typical of Mexican pueblos at the time:

34. John C. Cremony, *Life Among the Apaches* (1868).
35. John G. Bourke, *On The Border With Crook* (1902).

low adobe houses clustered around the plaza; streets that led away from the center of the village were narrow and dusty; women of all ages went about with heads covered with *rebozos* (scarves); beauty-conscious younger ones had their faces coated with flour paste, the "cosmetic of the southwest," to protect their delicate skin from the sun's rays; men were ambling about wearing cotton serapes and wide-brimmed sombreros; and dogs, chickens, and pigs meandered freely through the alleys and streets. As Bourke notes, "streets and pavements there were none; lamps were unheard of; drainage was not deemed necessary . . . There was no hint in history of a tradition of sweeping the streets, which were every bit as filthy as those in New York."[36]

Tucson collected enough votes and political clout to take the territorial capital away from Prescott in 1867. The old pueblo remained the capital of the Arizona Territory until it was restored to Prescott in 1877. Twelve years later, however, the capital was given a permanent location in Phoenix, much to the chagrin of Tucsonians who believed the distinction legitimately belonged to their city.

In 1873 Tucson was linked to the outside world by telegraph; eight years later, the telephone arrived. On March 20, 1880, the Southern Pacific Railroad stretched its steel rails eastward to Tucson. The arrival of the Iron

36. Ibid.

*Back in the days before electric trolleys, mules
hauled passengers through the streets of Tuscon. Here
the camera caught a wild-cat strike in the making.*

Horse was a great day for that "outpost of civilization," which had remained isolated and tormented by hostile Apaches for so many years. It was a momentous occasion for the loyal inhabitants of the old pueblo, and a thrilled mayor sent telegrams to the President of the United States, the governor of Arizona, and a host of other dignitaries, cheerfully proclaiming that Tucson was at last linked with the outside world. To make certain that no one of importance was overlooked, some wag suggested that the pope also be notified of the historic event. Acting on this advice, Mayor Leatherwood had the following message penned:

"To His Holiness, the Pope of Rome, Italy:

The mayor of Tucson begs your honor of reminding Your Holiness that this ancient and honorable pueblo was founded by the Spaniards under the sanctions of the Church more than three centuries ago, and to inform Your Holiness that a railroad from San Francisco, California, now connects us with the entire Christian world.

R.N. Leatherwood, Mayor, Asking your benediction. J.B. Salpointe Vic. Ap."

It was never quite clear whether or not the pope received the telegram, or if a reply was ever received. However, a few pranksters, learning of the telegram to the pope, crafted a reply of their own. After forging the

110

Pope's signature to the spurious message, they sent it to his honor, the Mayor. It read:

"His Holiness the Pope acknowledges with appreciation receipt of your telegram informing him that the ancient City of Tucson at last has been connected by rail with the outside world, and sends his benediction, but for his own satisfaction would ask—where in hell is Tucson? Antonelli. "

The telegram to the pope and the spurious reply became a much-repeated joke among the early pioneers of Tucson.

6 MEXICAN ARIZONA

> The brief history of Mexican Arizona can only
> be understood as a desperate seesaw for sur-
> vival. The Apaches would attack; the Mexi-
> cans would counterattack . . .
> —Thomas E. Sheridan, from *Arizona, A History*

From the turn of the nineteenth century until the end of Spanish rule in New Spain, European power struggles played a greater and more frequent role in shaping the course of events in Pimeria Alta than had previously been the case. These events more or less began in 1808, when Spain's ruling aristocracy became the unwilling hosts to an army of French troops, who dispossessed them of their monarch, and proclaimed Napoleon's brother Joseph their king. In New Spain this alarming chain of events aroused conflicting senti-ments. To many of the native-born Mexicans (criollos), intensely hostile toward their peninsular[37] leaders, it

37. Spanish-born.

was finally the moment to grab the reins of power and establish an independent Mexico. Throughout the provinces, a whole network of criollo groups plotted for independence; opposing them were the powerful Spanish overlords who ran the government, army, and church. From the time that Napoleon upset the Spanish monarchy, New Spain's criollo and peninsular factions challenged each other for dominance. In Mexico City, two viceroys were brought down in rapid succession by coup d'état.

Mexico's struggle for separation from the motherland actually began on September 16, 1810, when Father Miguel Hidalgo led a rebellion to free his country from colonial rule. Haplessly, not everyone went along. Though Hidalgo was killed and his rebellion crushed, the Hidalgo Revolt planted the seeds of change. After a decade of bloody encounter that followed, Mexico won its independence from Spain in 1821. A republic was founded in 1824. In that same year, the Territory of Nuevo Mexico was formed, including what are now the states of Arizona and New Mexico. Its capital at Santa Fe numbered 4,500 inhabitants, and its fertile eastern lands (present-day New Mexico) accounted for many cattle ranches. In marked contrast, all the ranches in the western portion (present-day Arizona) had been abandoned, leaving only the settlements of Tubac and Tucson, each guarded by a small garrison.

Throughout the early years of the young republic, just about every institution that had held the Spanish frontier together disintegrated as the country plunged into civil war and bankruptcy. In 1824, Mexico dismembered the Spanish colonial system and partitioned itself into states, including the state of Occidente.[38] This state comprised Sonora and Sinaloa, together with the settled areas around Tucson and Tubac. These territorial divisions frequently acted independently of one another in military affairs.[39] The Federal Congress passed a law in 1827 that expelled all Spaniards from the country. In conformity with the national law, several states enacted similar legislation. Under pressure from large landholders, the government confiscated church lands and auctioned them to the highest bidder.

The clergy were required to take a loyalty oath to Mexico, and all foreign-born padres were expelled. Captain Pedro Villaescusa was the commandant of Tucson, when he issued orders announcing the expulsion of the padres in his district. Reportedly he wept, as his predecessor Captain Juan de Anza had sixty-one years earlier, when he announced the Jesuit expulsion order to Father de Roxas. As later told by the Franciscans, Captain Villaescusa arrived outside the convent of San Ignacio during Holy Week 1828 with the expulsion order for his friend Fray Juan Vano, the Father President. Embarrassed to enter, he waited until Vano

---

38. In 1831, the Federal Congress approved the division of the Occidente into two separate states of Sinaloa and Sonora. Arizpe won the honor of being the state capital.

39. Thomas E. Sheridan, *Arizona, A History* (1995).

appeared. The padre consoled the captain, telling him that as a soldier he must do his duty. A short time later, Captain Villaescusa rode to Tumacacori to inform Fray Ramon Liberos that he must leave. He was given three days to arrange his affairs and depart. "What about the mission's property, livestock, stores, and tools?," Liberos inquired. Frankly, Villaescusa could not say and answered: "the comandante de armas had ordered the removal of the missionaries, no more no less."[40]

Never again would the missions be fully manned; the day of the resident missionary-protector had passed. The mission Indians were also living in mounting anticipation of Apache attack. The missions and settlements of Pimeria Alta separated into two divisions under two spiritual leaders. Father Perez Llera was given San Ignacio, Tubutama, Oquitoa, and Caborca, with their visitas. To Father Diaz went Tumacacori and Cocospera, and his old mission of San Xavier, together with the presidios of San Cruz, Tubac, and Tucson.

During the revolutionary years, peace agreements with the Apaches were ignored. By the mid-1830s, war parties once again swooped down on Tubac and Tucson. Seventy-five years had elapsed since the Franciscans had assumed charge of the Pimeria Alta Missions, when the last two padres withdrew from Pimeria Alta in 1842. But their success among the Indians was relatively fruitless

---

40. John Kessel, *Friars, Soldiers and Reformers: Hispanic Arizona and the Sonora Mission Frontier* (1976).

compared to those of the vigorous Jesuit mission communities of the early 1700s. They had not founded a single new mission.

During the turmoil of the revolutionary years, the silver mining industry was abandoned; the national treasury was almost depleted; and along the northern frontier, funds that had maintained missions, presidios, and Apache peace camps dried up. Apache raiding broke out again due to the Mexican government's failure to continue the policy of gathering and giving rations to Apache bands around presidios. By the mid-1830s, southern Arizona, with the exception of Tucson, was pretty much controlled by the Apaches. The once beautiful missions became deserted and fell into disrepair.

The Sonoran government, in a frantic move to stop Apache attacks on settlers, decided in 1835 on a war of extermination by offering one hundred pesos for each warrior's scalp turned in. Two years later, the Chihuahuan government added to a similar offer for a warrior, fifty pesos for a woman's scalp, and twenty-five for that of a child. The program, called *Projecto de Guerra*,[41] attracted an assortment of bloodthirsty ruffians who organized into units and rode into Apacheria in search of their "quarry." This genocidal crusade continued at a vigorous pace throughout the 1830s, although, at times, bounty funds were in short supply to pay for all the scalps being brought in. No one really knows how many

41. Project of War.

117

Apaches were killed by the scalp hunters; but the policy, barbaric and immoral as it was, served only to intensify the savagery and make the Apache warriors more relentlessly warlike.

Some Anglo-American trappers and traders entered into this trade along with the Mexicans. Unconscionably, they found it more lucrative to "trap for hair than for fur," and, as one wag put it, "caring naught whether they scalped the Mexicans themselves." Any scalp, recognizable as Indian, or otherwise, brought the pledged bounty. It was a time of treachery, violence, bloodshed, and a recurrence of savage Apache warfare.

Anglo-American Interlopers

The first Anglo-American intruders into Arizona arrived in 1824, not as an invading army, but as parties of trappers and hunters that operated from their headquarters in Taos, New Mexico. They were, as historian Thomas E. Sheridan so aptly described them, a ragtag collection of misfits, adventurers, and businessmen who entered Arizona for one purpose and one purpose only: to trap the "hairy banknotes," as they called beavers, from every watercourse between the upper Gila and the Colorado delta.[42]

---

42. Thomas E. Sheridan, *Arizona, A History* (1995).

Two of the first to set foot in the wilderness regions of Arizona were James Pattie and his father, Sylvester, who spent the winter of 1825–26 trapping along the San Francisco, Gila, and San Pedro Rivers. They had left their family farm in Kentucky in 1824 and headed for St. Louis, where they outfitted themselves for a fur-trapping expedition. They arrived in Taos, New Mexico in the fall of 1825. Before they headed into Arizona territory in search of beaver pelts, they had to secure permission and a Mexican license. They encountered a temporary delay in obtaining the license. The Mexicans, it seems, were becoming increasingly hostile at the increasing number of "buck-skin" Yankees entering their territory in search of pelts. In 1826, Santa Fe Mexican officials issued licenses to more than a hundred Anglo-American trappers to trap along the Gila River, but soon thereafter began placing limits on the number they issued.

Meanwhile, the Patties and their friends followed the Rio Grande south to Socorro, then headed west to the Santa Rita del Cobre Mines—the last outpost of Spanish civilization. They then rested before going into the rugged Gila hinterland. Trapping along the Gila, St. Francisco, and San Pedro Rivers, they collected several thousand dollars worth of pelts, which they hauled back to Santa Fe.

During the winter of 1826–1827, James Pattie returned to Arizona to join a group of French trappers led by Miguel Robidoux, one of six brothers who had grown up trapping along the Missouri River. Together, they journeyed down the Gila to the junction of the Salt and Gila Rivers, where they stopped at a village of Spanish-speaking Papagos. According to some sources, they may have been Yavapais or Tonto Apaches. The villagers invited the trappers to stay the night and, with the exception of a suspicious Pattie who camped some distance away, all accepted. As Pattie tells it, that evening the natives turned their war clubs on their guests, killing all the trappers, except himself, Robidoux, and an unidentified Frenchman.

Fleeing the massacre, the three stumbled upon the camp of another group of trappers led by Ewing Young. Young, a hard-bitten mountain man who it is said feared neither man nor beast, led his men back to the village where they exacted revenge. According to Pattie, when it was all over, more than one hundred Indians were slaughtered. Pattie remained with Young's outfit for the rest of the season, trapping up and down the Salt and Verde Rivers, and then following the Gila to Yuma Crossing, becoming the first Anglo-Americans to make the trek.

In 1830, James Pattie returned to his old Kentucky home, where he related astonishing stories of his encounters with Arizona's "fierce" human and animal inhabitants: battling with grizzlies, mountain lions, and Apaches; braving Comanche arrows to rescue naked women; and surviving a harrowing desert ordeal.

Three years earlier, his father Sylvester had died in a San Diego jail. As James tells the story, Sylvester joined his son's expedition in the fall of 1827. They trapped the Gila all the way to Yuma Crossing, where the local natives proved hostile and took away their horses. Undaunted, they loaded their furs onto canoes and headed down the Colorado River. At the mouth of the Colorado, they found more hostile Indians and, in a last frantic effort to escape, they headed west to the California coast. But ill luck still stalked them. When they arrived, they were arrested as trespassers and thrown in jail. Sylvester, very ill from the desert ordeal, died in his cell. Embellishing his story, James tells how he arranged for his release by promising to vaccinate "thousands" of locals from smallpox.

Other trappers may have preceded the Patties, and many certainly followed them, venturing into the unexplored valleys and mountains of Arizona in pursuit of a living, trapping and hunting. Fortunately, no other encounter between mountain men and Indians measured up to the horror of the Robidoux Massacre or its revenge. Still, there were frequent encounters as mountain men trekked through Apacheria, or trapped beaver in Mojave territory along the Colorado. To the Native Americans, they were armed intruders who had entered their lands without permission in order to snatch beavers from their rivers and streams. As their numbers increased, bands of Apache and Yavapai warriors intensified their resistance to these incursions. By the mid-1830s, most mountain men were avoiding Apacheria.

Relations between mountain men and Apaches reached a new low on April 22, 1837. This date saw James Johnson, an Anglo living in Sonora and a part-time scalp hunter, touch off the assassination of Juan Jose Compa and the slaughter of some of his followers.[43] Juan José was an influential and capable Mimbreño Apache leader, who had studied for the priesthood. His father had been murdered by Mexicans and, ever after, he was hostile toward them. Johnson, married to a Mexican woman, operated a trading post at Oposura in Sonora. Of the many versions of what happened that ill-fated night, the version given by Ben Wilson (who later became the first mayor of Los Angeles) is believed to be the most credible.

Wilson, who first met Juan Jose while trapping on the Gila in 1835, relates how he and a party of Missourians had gone into Sonora to purchase mules, only to find that the Apaches had stripped the countryside of them. En route home, they stopped off at Johnson's trading post, where they accepted an invitation from Johnson to accompany him and a friend named Glisson to Juan Jose's village. Arriving at the village, Johnson told the chief that he had brought along a sack of cornmeal for his people. While the cornmeal was being

---

43. Dan L. Thrapp, *The Conquest of Apacheria* (1967).

doled out, Glisson asked Juan Jose outside under the pretense of examining a sick mule. No sooner had they left than Johnson opened fire with a howitzer, killing and wounding many of the unsuspecting Apaches gathered around the sack for a share of the cornmeal. Outside, Glisson pulled a gun on Juan Jose, but did not kill him outright. As Juan Jose raised his knife to strike back, Johnson stole up behind and shot him dead. The young Mimbreño warriors counterattacked, killing many of the innocent Missourians, while Johnson and Glisson escaped unscathed. At least twenty Apaches, many of them women and children, died in the shooting.

This hideous crime brought about a new and vicious cycle of reprisals throughout Apacheria. It turned Mangas Coloradas, a relative of Juan José, into an enemy of the white man. Under the leadership of this son of an Apache warrior and a Mexican woman, the Mimbreños embarked on a path of bloodshed and destruction, wiping out trapping expeditions and even forcing the abandonment of the Santa Rita Mines. That cycle accelerated during the 1830s, and reached its zenith the following decade, when the only non-Indian communities in Arizona were the presidio at Tucson and the town of Tubac. By the 1830s, Tucson was as much an Apache as a Mexican community. According to the Sonoran census of 1831, Tucson had 465 Mexican residents; whereas four years later, the population of the Apache

Mangas, son of Mangas Colorado, the legendary Apache chieftain who died in 1863.

Manso community was said to include 486 individuals.[44] Tubac had to be abandoned in 1848.

Through the 1850s, Apache raiding became more frequent and extensive than it ever had before. Forays reached Tucson and even west of the Santa Cruz River, well into Papagos country. The Mexicans seemed powerless, as had the Spaniards before them, to formulate any lasting mechanism for bringing about peace with the Indians. This was the predicament the Americans faced when they took over control of southern Arizona in 1854.[45]

For several years after the revolution had begun, Mexico experienced one unstable government after another, until one man, Antonio Lopez de Santa Anna, finally wrested control of the government and entrenched himself as president-dictator. In 1835, he returned the country to a strong central government, usurping some of the powers that individual states, including Texas, had enjoyed since the revolution. This worsened relations between American colonists in Texas and the Mexican government and led to the United States-Mexican War, as well as to the subsequent acquisition of the Southwest from Texas to California. The Spaniards had long been haunted by the dread that other European powers were plotting to invade their sparsely populated

---

44. Thomas E. Sheridan, *A History of the Southwest* (1998).
45. Edward H. Spicer, *Cycles of Conquest* (1997).

northern frontier, but for the Mexicans who had won independence from Spain, it was the United States that made those fears a reality.

Mexican-American War

The war with Mexico began in May 1846, but its seeds were sown in 1824 when Mexico invited Anglo-Americans and other foreign colonists to settle the sparsely populated lands of Texas. So successful was the colonization that, by the mid-1830s, the ratio of Anglos to Mexicans was ten to one, and when a group of colonists seized a Mexican fort at Anahuac, the move for separation from Mexico had already begun. Vastly outnumbered, the Mexicans of Texas soon became a scorned minority in their native land.

In 1836, a group of settlers met and adopted a declaration of independence from Mexico and, shortly thereafter, defeated a Mexican army under Santa Anna at the Battle of San Jacinto. The settlers immediately ratified their own constitution, elected Sam Houston as President, and sent an envoy to Washington to seek annexation to the United States or recognition as the independent Republic of Texas. Texas remained an independent republic until 1845, when efforts to annex it to the United States were finally achieved.

In the meantime, President Polk, hoping to acquire the land from Texas to California by diplomatic negotiation with Mexico, sent John Slidell to Mexico City to negotiate the purchase of New Mexico and California and the vast land between the two (present-day Arizona). When the Mexican government refused to negotiate, President Polk proclaimed a state of war between the two neighbors. On March 28, 1846, General Zachary Taylor moved troops onto Mexican territory to the left bank of the Rio Grande in Mexican territory.

Hostilities began when Mexican troops crossed the Rio Grande on April 25 and inflicted casualties on a United States reconnaissance party in a cavalry skirmish. The Battle at Resaca de la Palma on May 9 ended in a rout of the Mexicans. Further attacks by Mexican forces led to the blockade of Mexican ports on the Pacific Ocean and the Gulf of Mexico. An army under General Winfield Scott was sent to Vera Cruz by sea with orders to advance on Mexico City. A second army under General Zachary Taylor entered Mexico from Texas; while a third army, the so-called "Army of the West" under the command of Colonel Stephen Watts Kearny, was ordered to take Santa Fe and then march to California.

Kearny's army consisted of three hundred regular cavalry, eight hundred rowdy, undisciplined but tough volunteers from Missouri, and a battalion of Mormons whose mission was to build a road across Arizona to California. The Army of the West followed the Santa Fe Trail to Bent's Fort on the Arkansas River. There, Kearny met up with several hundred wagons loaded with merchandise waiting to join him on the trek to Santa Fe (Santa Anna had earlier closed the trade route into Santa Fe).

An adroit Kearny sent one of his officers, Captain Phillip St. George Cooke, ahead to explore dialogue with New Mexico's governor Manuel Armijo and, according to some sources, to bribe him with hard cash. This might explain why Armijo and his force of dragoons had conveniently fled to Chihuahua by the time Kearny arrived. The Army of the West, warmly received by Lieutenant Governor Vigil, entered Santa Fe on August 18, 1846 without a single shot being fired. The American flag was raised over the *palico* of the governor; five weeks later, on September 22, Kearny issued a proclamation declaring American civil government in the Territory of New Mexico (which then included present-day Arizona) and the appointment of territorial officials.

The war with Mexico ended in 1848 with a treaty signed at Guadalupe Hidalgo, near Mexico City. Mexico agreed to give up its claims to Texas and ceded nearly half of her territory to the United States, including California, Arizona, New Mexico, Nevada, Utah, and Colorado. Much of the new international boundary in Arizona was north of the Gila River, leaving the route to California, constructed by the Mormon Battalion, running through Mexican territory. This, along with an international boundary dispute near El Paso, Texas, nearly led to open warfare between the two belligerents.

President Pierce sent James Gadsden to Mexico City in 1853 with an offer to purchase additional territory from Mexico, which the United States believed it needed for a southern route to connect the lower Mississippi Valley to California.

The first plan was to purchase all the land south of the Gila that is now Arizona and part, if not all, of Sonora in order to include the port of Guaymas on the Gulf of California, plus all of Baja California. The offered price of

James Gadsden, U.S. Minister to Mexico, negotiated the treaty that gave Arizona the land from the Gila River south to the present-day border with Mexico.

twenty million dollars was attractive to a Mexico in dire need of cash. The project, however, ran into trouble, not as had been expected with the Mexican authorities, but with Congress. Cognizant of the looming breach between North and South, senators and congressmen from northern states were not willing to see huge territories such as Sonora and Baja California acquired by the federal government, believing that such acquisition favored an expanding southern economy and the culture of slavery all the way to the Pacific Coast. Moreover, if a railroad was to reach the Pacific, the northern adherents wanted it in northern territory, west from Council Bluffs rather than west from New Orleans.

The debate in Congress continued until a compromise was finally reached. The border was set where it is today, allowing ample room for a wagon road and a railroad to cross Arizona south of the Gila to California. The price, ten million dollars, was accepted by Mexico, and on December 30, 1853, the Gadsden Purchase became a reality. To the American public, it was a seemingly useless expenditure: the ever-ready critics derided Congress for being so dumb as to buy a worthless desert. The Gadsden Purchase was considered absurd by much of the press, which often referred to the purchased tract as "our national cactus garden" and "rattlesnake heaven."[46]

And so it came about in 1854 that the southern boundary of Arizona was established at its present location. All of New Mexico south of the thirty-fourth parallel, plus the land between New Mexico and California (Arizona), were now part of the United States of America and became known as the Territory of New Mexico. Tucson and Tubac—with a population of

---

46. Edwin Corle, *The Gila* (1951).

about one thousand and three hundred, respectively—were the only towns of any consequence in the western part of the territory. The Gila Valley and virtually its entire watershed were under the Stars and Stripes. A route to the west was now assured; the boundary issue settled; an immense area was now available for settling; and untold wealth in mineral rights lay ready for the grabbing. But the United States also acquired something they had not bargained for—the hostile Apache Indians.

7

THE UNITED STATES
TERRITORY OF ARIZONA

"The best advice I can offer is to notify all settlers and miners to get out of Arizona and then withdraw the troops and leave the country to the tribes as a perpetual Indian territory where they can plunder and kill, each to their hearts' content."

—General William Tecumseh Sherman

It became evident shortly after the signing of the Gadsden Purchase Treaty that the Territory of New Mexico was too large and unmanageable for it to be efficiently administered, and that a breakup was necessary. Tucson, the largest city in the Gadsden Purchase area, was two hundred and fifty miles from the county seat at Mesilla, and more than five hundred miles by stage from Santa Fe, the territorial capital. Hence the citizens of the Santa Cruz Valley, for the most part, made and administered their own laws.

As early as 1856, Congress had been petitioned to set up a separate territory for Arizona, and several bills introduced toward this end had failed passage. Most of the early plans suggested for an "Arizona Territory" would have embraced only the southern parts of present-day Arizona and New Mexico, leaving out the unsettled reaches north of the Gila River, where no white settlements had yet existed. Hoping to goad Congress into speedier action, a provisional government was formed at a Tucson convention in April 1860. Delegates drew up a constitution that they believed would accommodate the area until the federal government created an official Arizona Territory. Moreover, the convention elected the region's first governor, Dr. Lewis S. Owings, a young physician turned gold miner.

The provisional convention reasserted Arizona's unyielding push to send a delegate of its own choosing to Congress. Four years earlier, in 1856, the residents had selected Nathan P. Cook as their delegate, but Washington rejected him. Nevertheless, Arizonans stubbornly persisted and elected Sylvester Mowry—a West Point graduate and successor to Samuel P. Heintzelman as commander at Fort Yuma—as their representative from 1857 through 1859 to plead their case for statehood with Congress.[47] But the pre-Civil War struggle over slavery precluded the formation of any new political units, and the question of separation of New Mexico into two territories lay dormant until the Republican

47. Bert M. Fireman, *Arizona: Historic Land* (1982).

Sylvester Mowry—flamboyant ex-army officer, mining entrepreneur, and promoter for Arizona's status as a territory.

Party gained control of Congress. The creation of new territories and states, likely to be loyal to the Union, then emerged as part of the overall strategy.

The Civil War, in a secondary way, aided Arizona's cause by bringing about a rivalry for control of the Southwest. The newly established Confederate government in Richmond served as a fomenter for action in Washington by creating its own blueprint for an "Arizona Territory"—one that comprised the southern segment of New Mexico between Texas and California. Faced with this threat to the Union, the House of Representatives passed the Organic Act. After deletion of a clause that would have placed the capital in Tucson, where Southern sympathies were known to prevail, the bill then cleared the Senate on February 20, 1863.

Four days later, President Lincoln signed the bill and the Territory of Arizona, including the Gadsden Purchase area, was created from the western portion of New Mexico. The proposed name of Gadsdenia was rejected in favor of Arizona, which had been in use for several years. The act provided for the establishment of a territorial government to remain in place "until such time as the people residing in said territory shall, with the consent of Congress, form a State government and apply for admission into the Union as a State, on an equal footing with the original States."

Most of this new land acquired from Mexico was known only to a few fearless mountain men, who had earlier traversed the area's mountains and deserts in search of furs. So one of the first tasks for the United States government was to survey and map routes for transporting passengers and freight. This responsibility was assigned to the Army Corps of Topographical Engineers, a specialized cadre of audacious explorer-scientists. The first of these daring explorers was Captain Lorenzo Sitgreaves who, in 1851, led an expedition of twenty men with an escort of soldiers. Guided by the legendary scout Antoine Leroux, the party traveled along the thirty-fifth parallel. Along the way, they were attacked first by Yavapai warriors and then by Yuma Indians before reaching Fort Yuma, totally fatigued from their ordeal. Two years later, Lieutenant A.W. Wipple led a small survey party across the north-central portion of Arizona westward from Zuni, New Mexico to Cajon Pass, California. There were other expeditions as exploration of the vast new territory continued through the 1850s, but none compared to the expedition led by Edward F. Beale.

In 1855, Congress commissioned Secretary of War Jefferson Davis to forge a supply route from Texas to California across Arizona, while at the same time appropriating thirty thousand dollars for the project. Davis turned to the camel, the pack animal best equipped to carry large loads across the desert with minimum need for water and food. They were used successfully in the Middle East and in North Africa, so why not use them in the desert of the Southwest. To carry out the task, he picked an adventurer named

Edward Fitzgerald Beale a lieutenant in the Topographical Engineers.[48] Beale sent Major Henry Wayne to the Middle East with a wad of greenbacks to purchase some thirty camels. A navy ship, transporting the animals from the Middle East to the United States, arrived in 1856 in Texas, where the camels were unloaded and assigned a driver.

There was no doubt that the camels' amazing ability to go great distances without water, eating only the natural forage along the trail, could offer a solution to the army's Southwestern transportation hurdle, but only if the hired hands, most of whom were former muleskinners, could learn to communicate with the exotic beasts. As one wag described it, "the hired hands couldn't speak Arabic and the headstrong beasts wouldn't learn English." The dilemma was partly solved when the army imported two North African camel drivers, who set about instructing the former muleskinners on how to cope with their new traveling companions and to communicate with them in their native tongue. But there was still the problem of the camel's foul breath and their strange habit of spitting at anyone they didn't like, which the muleskinners had a difficult time getting used to.

Beale was successful in opening up his wagon route, but this romantic episode in Arizona's history came to an

---

48. Beale was a hero of the Battle of San Pascual, where he slipped through Mexican lines to reach San Diego and direct sailors to the rescue of General Kearny's crippled army.

Lieutenant Edward F. "Ned" Beale. A colorful adventurer, he led the fabled camel survey across northern Arizona in the 1850s

end when the Civil War arrived. Troops were withdrawn from the Southwest and the project was abandoned. In time a few of the camels were sold as pack animals, but the majority were simply allowed to escape into the desert. For many years thereafter, they could be observed wandering in the foothills around the Gila and Columbia Rivers. Over the course of time, some were shot, some were captured, and the rest simply disappeared.

Travel in Arizona prior to the area's acquisition from Mexico had been essentially in the north-south direction: the Spaniards pushing north from Mexico City, seeking treasure to take back with them and souls to convert; while the Indian bands made their living by raiding southward to the frontiers of settlement. East-west routes began opening up following the Guadalupe Hidalgo Treaty, and overland travel through Arizona to California increased steadily. Stagecoaches began arriving in 1857 with the opening of the San Antonio-San Diego Mail Line. Dubbed the "Jackass Mail," its passengers had to exchange their coach seats for a saddle mule over part of the desert journey. The following year, the leather-slung coaches of John Butterfield's Overland Mail began a spectacular twenty-six day run from St. Louis, through Tucson and Yuma, to San Francisco. It had to be shut down only once in its thirty-month history, when Cochise and his Chiricahua Apaches went on the warpath near Apache Pass.

From 1852 until the Southern Pacific Railroad was completed from the west coast to Yuma in 1878, many

Paintings by Tombstone artist Marjorie Reed that depict the legendary Butterfield Overland Mail, which operated in Arizona from 1858 to 1861. Top: *Changing Horses and Coach at Gila Bend. Bottom: Colorado River Crossing.* (PHOTO: GARY M. JOHNSON)

passengers and supplies were carried in sea-going vessels through the Gulf of California and transferred to smaller vessels for transport to ports along the Colorado River. Yuma, 175 miles up the Colorado, was the dock for southern Arizona; passengers and freight bound for Prescott, Wickenberg, or other locations in central Arizona were unloaded at La Paz or Ehrenburg.

During the years preceding the Civil War, four military posts were established in Arizona. The first, at Fort Yuma on the California side of the Yuma Crossing, was established on October 2, 1848. Getting supplies to the base in this remote location was a problem during the first four years of operation; they had to be hauled overland across the hazardous desert from San Diego. Then, in 1852, the first steamboat carrying supplies succeeded in making its way up the Colorado River, and the future of the base was secured. A second base, Fort Defiance, was built at Four Corners in 1851 to keep an eye on the Navajos, who for generations had raided the Hopi and Spanish settlements along the Rio Grande. It was dubbed "Hell's Gate" by the soldiers stationed there: its location made it vulnerable to attacks on three sides. In 1856, a third base was established as Fort Buchanan to protect the settlers and miners in the mountains south of Tucson. Three years later, Fort Mojave was built on the Colorado River as a shelter for travelers following the old Beale Camel Road across northern Arizona.

Steamboats on the Colorado River. From the 1850s to the 1880s, steamboats were the main mode of travel to and from Arizona.

Fort Defiance (1860), the first U.S. military fort in Arizona, was established as a base of operations against the Navajo. (SKETCH: JOSEPH HEGER, 1860)

Charles D. Poston: Self-Styled Father of Arizona

Among the earliest pioneers who came from the east soon after the Gadsden Purchase was Charles D. Poston, an enterprising character who went on to play a significant role in the territory's development. His adventures and exploits are a metaphor for life as experienced in Arizona's embryonic years. News of the Gadsden Purchase launched Poston on a journey of intrigue and adventure involving Mexican land grants, railroad routes from the Mississippi to the Pacific, and lost silver mines. He was a gregarious, persuasive, and daring Kentuckian who studied law and went west to California in the Gold Rush. From 1851 to 1853, he was the chief clerk in the San Francisco Customs House and dabbled in real estate on the side.

Charles D. Poston, called the "Father of Arizona" for his efforts in creating Arizona as a territory separate from New Mexico

Along the way, he met and became

friends with Christian Ehrenberg, a topographical engineer and surveyor. Together, they prospected the hills in Sonora and the Gadsden Purchase area. Poston returned to Kentucky in 1854 to visit his family, and from there headed to Washington and New York to muster support and financing for the Sonora Exploring and Mining Company—an enterprise to be formed by he, Ehrenberg, and another friend, Major Heintzelman. In 1858, having successfully acquired the necessary financing for the venture, he and Ehrenburg headed west to develop the mines around Tubac. Although this was neither the first nor the only venture into the Gadsden Purchase by Anglo-Americans, it was the most spectacular and the best publicized. Both men had a talent for proclaiming their adventures.

Poston established his company's headquarters at the abandoned Mexican presidio in Tubac. The territory, as one historian described it, was in deepest limbo at the time. Many of the Mexicans had left, and the New Mexico government was far away in Santa Fe. "We had no law but love," wrote Poston in his memoirs, "and no occupation but labor. No government, no taxes, no public debt, no politics. It was a community in a perfect state of nature."[49]

In this frontier "utopia," where silver was being mined in the nearby Santa Rita Mountains, Poston proceeded to print his own Tubac paper money, known as

---

49. A.W. Gressinger, *Charles D. Poston – Sunland Seer* (1961).

boletas, on the same handpress from which he issued Arizona's first newspaper, the *Weekly Arizonian*. By 1858 Tubac's population had risen to eight hundred, as miners flocked in from south of the border. As the *alcalde* or magistrate in charge of all criminal and civil affairs of the community under the government of New Mexico, Poston took it upon himself to perform marriages, baptize children, grant divorces, execute criminals, and perform a host of other duties. Young couples who couldn't afford the twenty-five dollar fee charged by the priests in Sonora flocked to Tubac, where Poston not only married them for free, but gave them jobs in the mines as well.

In assuming the duties of the church as well as his other civic duties, Poston created many problems for himself. When Bishop Lame of New Mexico heard that he was marrying people and baptizing children, he sent his vicar apostolic, Father Mashhoeuf, to investigate. Father Mashhoeuf, having carefully surveyed the scene, took Poston aside one morning and discreetly told him, "My young friend, I appreciate all you have been trying to do for these people, but the marriages, baptisms and divorces you have performed are not good in the eyes of God."[50] Playing down his behavior, Poston told the vicar general, "I had not charged any of them anything and had given them a marriage certificate with a seal on it, made out of a Mexican dollar. . . ."[51] However, a

---

50. Ibid.
51. Ibid.

compromise was worked out that cost Poston a seven hundred dollar fee, and Father Mashhoeuf agreed to sanction all of the marriages and baptisms that Poston had performed.

In his memoirs, Poston describes how business rapidly grew in the pre-Civil War years in Tubac: "We had scarcely commenced to make silver bars . . . (when) pack trains arrived from Mexico loaded with all kinds of provisions."[52] He also mentions that cross border relations with Mexico were generally amiable until 1857, when a "filibustering party" of forty armed Californians, known as the Crabb Expedition, invaded Sonora. They were cornered in Caborca and wiped out, but the anger over the affair drove the Mexican government to impose restrictions on trade and cross-border traffic. When it became unsafe for persons of either nationality to cross the border, mining operations in the Santa Rita Mountains were temporarily halted.

As matters started to improve again and work renewed in the mines, Chiricahua Apaches went on the warpath and bands of plundering Apaches raided throughout the Santa Cruz Valley. That same year, the Civil War broke out and the United States government focused its attention on more compelling matters. Federal troops were removed from the region, and Forts Buchanan and Breckinridge were closed down.

---

52. Ibid.

Apache scouts.

Military-style family outing in the 1870s.

With the protective troops withdrawn, the Apaches moved in, carrying off the livestock, and reducing Tubac and surrounding installations to ruins. Armed Mexicans in considerable numbers crossed over the border, declaring that the American government had abandoned the area and that they had come to take their country back again. Poston's dream world was shattered as he tried to come to grips with the chain of events happening around him. Even the few Americans left in the territory, he later wrote, were at war among themselves.

Poston was in Washington when the pressure to make Arizona a separate territory was gathering momentum with Congress. The leaders of the Confederacy, with eyes on the mineral-laden mountains of southern Arizona and a link between Texas and California, were already moving to annex the southern part of New Mexico. In July of 1861, Lieutenant-Colonel John Baylor with three hundred Confederate soldiers moved into New Mexico from Texas and captured Mesilla. Early the next year, the Confederate Congress passed an enabling act annexing all the territory from Texas to California south of the thirty-fourth parallel; President Jefferson Davis promptly proclaimed it the Arizona Territory of the Confederate States. Baylor was appointed governor, and Mesilla was selected as its capital.

At the same time that the proclamation was issued, an assembly of Tucson residents, mostly of southern origin, passed an ordinance of secession. The Stars and

Stripes were removed; Granville Oury was selected territorial delegate to the Confederate Congress; and President Davis was petitioned for troops. Captain Sherod Hunter was sent west to occupy Tucson, arriving to a friendly reception on February 28, 1862. Most Tucsonians, beleaguered by Apache attacks, were happy to see soldiers no matter what the color of the uniform. With no Union soldiers to confront, Hunter campaigned against the Apaches.

Very soon, a Union counter attack was on its way. A 2,000-man force led by Colonel James H. Carleton set out from California toward Arizona. At the old Butterfield Overland Stage stop known as Stanwix Station on the Gila River (about eighty miles east of Yuma), scouts from Hunter's party encountered outriders from Carleton's force. Several shots were fired, and a Union soldier was wounded before the two patrols dispersed. Stretching the point a bit, some claim this skirmish to be the westernmost battle of the Civil War.

A healthier case can be made for the skirmish that took place a few days later at Picacho, where Lieutenant Jim Barrett surprised three Confederate soldiers and took them prisoner, then negligently allowed his own men to be ambushed. An intense ninety-minute fight ensued, and when the smoke had cleared, Barrett and two of his men were dead and three were wounded. Two Confederate soldiers would later die from the wounds they received. The Union force withdrew, and the Confederates headed back to Tucson where they

Battle of Picacho, April 15, 1862. (PHOTO: MARSHALL TRIMBLE)

informed Captain Hunter of the approaching California column. He gathered his hundred or so troops, lowered the colors, mounted up and rode east out of town.

On May 20, 1862, three Union columns positioned themselves for the re-capture of Tucson, which the Confederates had held since February. Only when they converged on the center of the city did they learn from the amused residents that the Rebels had already withdrawn. Arriving several days later, Carleton proclaimed martial law; made himself military governor of Arizona; dispatched soldiers to protect outlying mines; and ordered the arrest of mine owner Sylvester Mowry, formerly commander of Fort Yuma, on the charge of being a Southern sympathizer. Mowry was later exonerated, but in the meantime his mine had been sequestered and pillaged by Carleton's friends.

Throughout these skirmishes, Charles Poston and his friends in Washington were making progress with Congress for Arizona's separate territorial status. Even with President Lincoln's support, however, many legislators refused to sanction the bill. "O yes," said Senator Wade of Ohio when Poston dropped in on him, "I have heard of that country—it is just like hell. All it lacks is water and good society."[53] In 1863 the Territory of Arizona, carved out of the western part of New Mexico, finally became a reality. At the signing of the legislation, Poston presented President Lincoln with a sculpturesque inkstand of Santa Rita silver, bearing his name and Lincoln's.

John Goodwin arrived at Fort Whipple on January 22, 1864 as the first United States governor of the territory. For him and his aides, the job of organizing the new territory would require much energy and toil. The area was full of hostile Indians who roamed almost unchecked. Southern sympathizers, most opposed to the Washington appointees, concealed their views. The year before, discoveries of rich gold placers in the

---

53. Lawrence Clark Powell, *Arizona* (1976).

Bradshaw Mountains had opened the territory north of the Gila River to new settlers. But there were few laws, no institutions, no transportation, no mail service, and some officials were more interested in "striking it rich" than in dealing with the affairs of the community. Poston was appointed to represent the territory in Washington but was defeated at the hands of Governor Goodwin in the following year's regular election.

Escalation of Apache Hostilities

As federal troops marched east out of Arizona in 1861 to drive back the Confederate invasion of New Mexico, Indians mistakenly thought that they had finally succeeded in driving the white man out. That same year, a miscalculation by the military touched off what would become a long and ruthless war with the Apaches, known as the Bascomb Affair. There are varied versions of what led to the severing of friendly relations between Apache Chief Cochise and the Americans.

One rendition tells how Apaches raided the ranch of a John Ward and ran off with his son Felix and some of his cattle. Some would prefer to think that the boy ran away after a beating from his drunken father. Whichever was the case, Ward complained to Major Stein that the Indians had kidnapped his son, and Stein ordered a search party under a Lieutenant George Bascomb to retrieve the boy. Bascomb's men pursued some

Apaches into the mountains, where they called a parley and summoned the leaders to meet with them. Chief Cochise of the Chiricahuas and three other unsuspecting chiefs showed up only to be accused by Bascomb of kidnapping the boy. Cochise suggested to Bascomb that the White Mountain Apaches had taken the boy and promised to get him back within ten days. However, Bascomb advised Cochise that he and his friends were under arrest until the boy was returned.

Infuriated, Cochise slashed his way through the side of the tent where they stood talking, and propelled his way past the soldiers standing outside. Miraculously, he escaped with only a slight leg wound. Bascomb ignored Cochise's demand that his friends be released, and the Apaches then seized an employee of the Butterfield stage station. Cochise offered to exchange the prisoner for his people, and again Bascomb ignored his request. Two days later, Cochise burned a wagon train, killing nine Mexicans and taking four Americans prisoners. The bloody spiral accelerated and he next attacked Bascomb's command without success. Cochise then executed the four American prisoners he was holding hostage. Bascomb's men hung six Apache warriors in retaliation, including Cochise's brother and two nephews.

From the Ward incident, a bloody and treacherous war evolved between the American military and the Chiricahua Apaches. Many lives were lost, much property destroyed, and much agony inflicted on the lives of many innocent families. As one source put it, the cost of the war against Cochise and his warriors would have purchased John Ward a string of cattle stretching from the Atlantic to the Pacific.

National attention began to focus on the Indian dilemma in Arizona after the Aravaipa Apache massacre at Camp Grant. In 1871, a group of vigilantes—ninety-four Papago, forty-eight Mexicans and six Americans from the Tucson area—attacked a local band of Aravaipa Apache, nearly wiping out the group in a few furious moments. When the carnage was over, more than a hundred, mostly women and children, were dead. An outraged President Grant called the Camp Grant incident "murder" and ordered a trial. The trial, held in Tucson, not surprisingly brought in a "not guilty" verdict. Arizonans had been at the mercy of the fierce Apaches for years and, at that time, no jury in the Arizona Territory would find anyone guilty of killing an Apache.

Within a decade of the creation of the territorial government in 1863, Indians began to realize and embrace the inevitable consequence of the white man's preeminence in numbers and resources. In successive stages, they gathered at feeding stations or reservations. But as historian Bert M. Fireman pointed out, contradictory national policies precipitated constant turmoil that periodically led to outbreaks, murder, and pillage.

The Navajos encountered a similar situation. In 1864 Kit Carson held a meeting with their leaders near

Chinle that ended their long war with the Americans. Carson, ordered to conduct a war of extermination against the Navajos, chose instead to starve them into capitulation. Following a ruthless campaign in Canyons de Chelly and del Mueto, more than eight thousand Navajo surrendered and were taken on the infamous "long walk" to the Pecos River Reservation in New Mexico.

Cochise died in 1874, and the Chiricahua command void was soon occupied by a Bedonkohe Apache named Geronimo (after St. Jerome). A native of eastern Arizona, Geronimo had followed the great chief, Mangas Coloradas, to Mexico in 1850. He grew to hate Mexicans for they had killed his mother, wife, and three children. In fact, Geronimo was never a chief; he was a war leader.

In 1876, federal authorities rounded up several bands of Apaches, including Geronimo and his warriors. They were placed onto a reservation at San Carlos, described as "Hell's Forty Acres." The move proved unwise. The restive Apaches, especially the Chiricahua, abhorred reservation living and, to make matters worse, conditions on the reservation were appalling. Then came rumors that all Apaches would be moved to Oklahoma. It was only a matter of time before some incident or other would spark a riot. It came when the agency chief of police tried to arrest an Indian. The suspect ran and the officer fired into a crowd of people, killing a woman. The Chiricahua screamed for justice.

Geronimo, the legendary Chiricahua Apache war leader.

When it was not forthcoming, they waited for the opportune moment, then seized the police chief and beheaded him. Afterwards Geronimo, with several hundred of his people, bolted the reservation and fled into Mexico's Sierra Madre Mountains, where he resumed a life of raiding in the border areas of Mexico and the United States.

Overshadowed by other Apache headmen, Geronimo didn't emerge as a prominent leader until 1881, but would go on to be a legendary figure—a dreaded enemy and a scourge to ranchers and miners on both sides of the border. Mexicans accused Americans of not doing enough to prevent reservation Apaches from raiding at will into Sonora and Chihuahua. Americans, for their part, resented the fact that a pool of hostile Apaches remained more or less unmolested in the Sierra Madre Mountains. Finally, an agreement was negotiated whereby troops from either country in "hot pursuit" of Apache raiders could penetrate as deeply as necessary into the other nation. This cooperation was the beginning of the end of the Apache wars.

General George Crook was recalled to Arizona in 1882 to pursue Geronimo. During an earlier campaign in Arizona's central mountains, Crook had subdued the Yavapai and Tono Apaches in a matter of months. He began his campaign into the Sierra Madre Mountains in 1883, after receiving permission from the Republic of Mexico to cross the border. His army penetrated into the Indians' Sierra Madre's "natural

George Crook, called the "greatest Indian-fighting general" in the army. He was also one of the few to win the respect and trust of the Indians.

fortress," dealing the Chiricahua a psychological defeat. Crook's destroy-and-burn strategy forced the Chiricahua to negotiate. Crook's terms were precise: return to the reservation at once. They agreed and, within a few months, Geronimo and his people were back in San Carlos.

It was only a matter of time until Geronimo and his followers bolted from the reservation again, and once again Crook's men pursued them into the Sierra Madre Mountains. On March 25, 1886, a meeting took place at Canyon de los Embudos. Geronimo surrendered to Crook and his terms: two years exile for Geronimo and his band in Florida before being allowed to return to the reservation in San Carlos. After the chief gave several lectures on the injustices that his people had suffered at the hands of the white man, he agreed to the terms. Crook then headed back to his headquarters at Fort Bowie to wire the news to Washington, and the Indians started their journey back to the United States.

161

Military pack trains were essential to the success of the campaigns against the Apaches.

Along the way, Geronimo and several of his warriors bolted and returned to Mexico. According to his own account, he became suspicious that the soldiers were planning to kill him. "We were not under any guard at the time," he would later tell, "The United States troops marched in front and the Indians followed. I do not know how far the United States army had gone before they missed us." When word reached Washington of his escape, Crooke was replaced by General Nelson Miles.

Miles sent a trusted officer, Lieutenant Charles B. Gatewood, to seek his surrender and agreement to the previous terms. Exhausted and hopelessly outnumbered, Geronimo had little choice. He agreed and insisted on surrendering to General Miles personally; on September 4, 1886, the historic surrender took place at Skeleton Canyon, a few miles southeast of Geronimo Mountain. Geronimo and his Chiricahua followers were then shipped to a prison camp in Florida, where they spent not the promised two years but a full decade. Despite captivity, Geronimo rode in President Theodore Roosevelt's inaugural parade in 1905. He died in 1909 in Oklahoma without ever again setting foot in his native Arizona, where bitter memories of the Apache wars endured in the minds of the people—Anglo, Mexican, and Indian. They buried him in the Apache cemetery at Fort Sill.

In the land called "Apacheria," the Apaches had the upper hand for centuries—first in their wars with the Spaniards and later the Mexicans. But it would take the tenacity of the Americans to make the final conquest of the region possible, and it would take many years of tough guerrilla warfare to accomplish the feat. Historian Dan F. Trapp describes it more aptly than most: "The conquest of Apacheria, stained with the blood of thousands, and washed in the heroism and valor of men of different races, is an American saga and one that needs to be told. Through it was seized the last great block of continent to be made a part of the American commonwealth. Through it was resolved for all time the question of supremacy between aborigine and settler, white man and red. Through it was perpetuated grief and terror and bloody-handed savagery and nobleness until the inevitable was brought about, until the land was lost and made secure for the whites."[54]

54. Dan F. Thrapp, *The Conquest of Apacheria* (1967).

8 GROWTH AND PROGRESS IN THE TERRITORIAL YEARS

In the glorious spring of 1877, the astute old wagon master, John Meadows, gave a quick lash of his whip and bellowed, "Gidiyap," as they pulled out of Visalia one early morning, bound for the green pastures in the Tonto Basin of Arizona . . . The caravan disappeared into the dawn carrying with it the hopes and dreams of great opportunities in a promised land.

—From "Arizona Charlie—The Meadows Migrate to Arizona"

Throughout much of the territorial years, Arizona was anything but a nirvana as determined prospectors, farmers, ranchers, and soldiers braved the elements to endure the harsh realities of a frontier environment.[55] First came the burro prospector, attracted by the lure of gold and silver, who combed the mountainsides in search of precious metals. He opened up the

---

55 Beth Lucy, *Arizona at Seventy-Five* (1987).

country to the large mining outfits, merchants, ranchers, soldiers, and settlers who followed in his footsteps. Tent communities sprang up almost overnight in the remote regions where mineral deposits appeared. Many of them became towns, a few became cities, and others became ghost towns once the minerals were gone. Farmers and ranchers, lured to the grassy and well-watered valleys along the Santa Cruz and San Pedro Rivers, braved the ordeal of hostile Apaches. Shadier characters arrived to take advantage of the frontier's reputation for lawlessness. Between 1865 and 1886, people moved west by the thousands and, for whatever reason they came, the newcomers settled on traditional lands that belonged to the area's original inhabitants, the American Indians. This intrusion created conflict and many of the Indian groups—the Chiricahua Apaches and the Yavapai, in particular—strongly resisted it.

Within a generation after its acquisition, the United States moved forcibly into different parts of Arizona to exert preeminence over the native inhabitants. With their eventual subjugation and confinement on reservations, federal policy entered a new and significant phase toward the Indians. Some historians refer to this period as the "Americanization era." It began around 1860 and ended in the waning years of the 1920s, after the recommendations of a government study paved the way for far-reaching reforms of Indian relations.[56] Before the

---

56. "On the Problem of Indian Administration."

1870s, the few reservations in existence were administered by Army Officers, with a military presence intended to keep the Indians in submission. The Grant Peace Policy of 1871 introduced civil administration under the direction of the Bureau of Indian Affairs, placing the Indian's well-being under an agent of the Bureau.

The reservation idea came about as a program of United States policy in the 1860s. As a social fixture among the Arizona Indians, it did not fully emerge until perhaps the 1890s. Indian historian, Edward H. Spicer, describes it as the "superintendency," where the reservation was managed by a superintendent (an Indian agent) responsible to superiors in the Bureau of Indian Affairs in Washington, and without democratic participation by the Indians. It evolved into a paternal relationship, the consequences of which led to the decline of the Indians' tribal autonomy.

For example, the Gila Pimas had a functioning village organization little affected in any significant way throughout the Spanish colonial period. There were peace leaders and an organization of elders who managed the cultivation of crops and the irrigation system. They had a tribal leader to coordinate villages in warfare and, to some extent, in relations with the Spaniards. This form of village organization was functioning when Indian Bureau agents were placed among them in the 1880s. At the same time, the Pimas' agriculture economy became increasingly at risk with the loss of

Gila River irrigation water to a swelling number American farmers who were settling on their traditional lands. As the water crisis worsened, Indian Bureau personnel increasingly assumed responsibility over the Pimas' farming activities, dragging them into a dependent relationship with the federal government. As their dependency became more acute, the Pimas' traditional organizational structure and economic way of life degenerated; by the early twentieth century, it had plunged them into intense poverty and social instability.

A similar situation with analogous consequences took place when Apaches were herded onto the San Carlos Apache Reservation, where they were forced to adapt to a living mode greatly in contrast to their traditional nomadic food gathering and raiding style. To keep them from starving, the Bureau was compelled to issue them food rations, which ultimately led to their dependency on the federal government. In similar fashion, the Walapai, Havasupai, Yuma, Mojave-Chemehuevi, and Fort Apache Reservations developed dependent relationships.

The Navajos, on the other hand, escaped much of the influence of government supervision, mainly because of the undesirability of Navajo land to the colonists. They continued to live undisturbed in the northeastern corner of Arizona in social units of several extended families over a defined territory, within which they raised corn and herded sheep. They successfully resisted efforts by the Indian Bureau to introduce government programs. The Papagos, living in rancherias spread over a wide area (except for a few hundred at the village of San Xavier), escaped government supervision for a generation longer than any other tribe, until a reservation was created for them 1917.

In 1934 the Indian Reorganization Act, passed by Congress, organized the reservation as a political unit for the first time. The Apache, Papago, Pima, and Yuman tribes promptly organized tribal councils and began to deliberate and to take action on reservation affairs under the aegis of constitutions. The councils provided some voice in the running of reservation affairs, but superintendents still held final power of deciding the important issues. The intent of this new policy was to develop Indian leadership; by 1945, transitional units were assuming more management responsibilities, particularly with respect to the handling of reservation law and order problems.

The Mining Industry

Arizona's first mining boom started with the discovery of the now famous Planchas de Plata near the tiny *rancheria* of Arissona in 1736. That boom was effectively ended by the Pima uprising of 1751, during which time, it has been suggested, the Indians filled in a great many Spanish mining tunnels and quite effectively obliterated most of the Spanish mines in Arizona. The re-establishment of Spanish authority in the area brought with it a growth in prosperity, mostly based upon mining activities in the mountains west of Tubac, in the Babocomari Valley and in the Santa Rita Mountains. During Mexico's war of independence from Spanish rule in the early 1820s, mining once again ceased, not to commence again on any notable scale until the Gadsden Purchase by the United States at the end of 1853. It was during this hiatus that the American mountain men made their excursions into Arizona and went prospecting and trapping. They mostly made their living from furs, although occasionally they collected some rich ore.

The period from 1854 through 1865, when the Civil War ended, saw the start-up of American mining activity in Arizona This development had a direct and consequential influence on both the politics and the citizenry of the territory. Many historians have written that if not for these early strikes, such as those by Poston and Hermann in the Santa Rita Mountains, Arizona would not have been made a separate territory. The end of the Civil War brought to Arizona a great influx of individuals, most of whom were seeking refuge and a new way of life far from the war-torn East. The years between 1865 and 1880 were so active with prospectors and miners that, according to geophysicists, most of Arizona's primary mineral discoveries were made during that time.

It was not until the military secured sections of Arizona from Indian raids that mining developed on a large scale. It was gold that attracted miners to Arizona in the 1860s; but from the mid-1870s to the mid-1880s, silver was king. Then copper took its place as the territory's most important mineral source. Copper had few uses until the 1880s, when it became important for new sources such as electric cables, telephone wires, and appliances.

In 1858, precisely a decade after the California gold rush, Arizona's first gold strike occurred at Gila City on the Gila River east of Yuma Crossing. Before its closure, the Gila City placer mine had produced enough of the coveted ore to proclaim Arizona as the new golden land. In 1862 an old mountain man, Pauline Weaver, turned up at a store near Yuma with a goose quill filled with golden flakes, which had been recovered from a sandy wash 150 miles upstream on the Arizona side of the Colorado River. He named the site La Paz and, by the time the strike was exhausted, miners had extracted more than eight million dollars worth of gold. It was at La Paz in 1862 that the legendary Goldwater family began its commercial business; Michael Goldwater, Senator Barry Goldwater's grandfather, opened a store there.

At the close of the Civil War campaign in Arizona, a former Confederate officer and deserter by the name of Jack Swilling and a well-known mountain man, Joseph Reddeford Walker, organized a prospecting trip

Pauline Weaver—mountain man, scout, and gold prospector. He was one of Arizona's most prominent trailblazers and is called "Prescott's first citizen."

A mule-team transporter hauling ore from a mine.

to the headwaters of the Hassayampa River. News of their rich placer finds along Granite, Lynx, Turkey, and a host of other creeks in the area is believed to have accelerated Lincoln's decision to confirm Arizona as a separate territory in February 1863. So substantial was the discovery that General Jim Carleton, then commandant of the military department of New Mexico, dispatched a company of soldiers to the wilderness area to protect the miners. Carleton appreciated the potential value of the mines to the Union cause, and took action to secure the Walker gold fields from Confederacy hands in June 1863.

He ordered a large expedition to establish Fort Whipple at a site near the Walker party. The location of Fort Whipple, and its availability to guard the new government of the territory, was a major determinant influencing the selection of the site (later Prescott) for the territorial capital by Governor Goodwin and his party. The location of the fort and of the capital also encouraged the growth of the area where, by 1865, there were at least three thousand placer mines being worked in the vicinity of Prescott.[57]

It soon became obvious that almost everywhere in Arizona there were hills and ridges rich in minerals. Two other important discoveries of the early 1860s were John Moss' mine near the site of the present town of Oatman in northwestern Arizona, and Henry Wickenburg's Vulture Mine. The Moss Mine was important not only in that it produced rich ore, but also because it served to focus attention on area that had been previously neglected. The Vulture Mine is said to have received its name from the fact that Henry Wickenburg, upon reaching down to pick up a rock to throw at a vulture, found it unusually heavy. Scratching around in the loose stones, he was amazed to find gold visible to the naked eye on a ledge thirty-feet wide.

In the decades following the Civil War, notwithstanding the lack of roads and the danger of frequent

---

57. Edward H. Peplow, *History of Arizona* (1958).

Indian attacks, miners and prospectors scoured the rugged mountains of Arizona in search of precious ore. Gold mining had started out relatively easy; the gold-seeker dipped his pan in water, carefully sifted the sand away and was left with the yellow stuff. This kind of mining was called "placer," and much of the Southwest was opened by gold-seekers intent on filling a small bag full of gold dust and moving on.

Placer gold ran out and, at that point, rock mining became a big business requiring huge capital investments. During the 1870s, the emphasis turned to silver and copper, when several substantial silver mines and at least one major copper deposit were discovered. These discoveries intensified interest in Arizona mining and brought in the venture capital needed to finance the cost of excavation, as well as the building of smelters necessary to prepare the ore for market.

Probably the richest single silver mine was at Silver King, near present-day Superior. It was first discovered by a soldier named Sullivan in 1871, during the construction of a military road. Soon after, Sullivan dropped out of sight, and it was thought that he had been killed by Indians on the way to file his claim. Four years later, a party of prospectors fortuitously came across the "Lost Sullivan Mine." According to one version of what happened, the prospectors got into a skirmish with a party of Apache and, during the heat of action, one of their burros ran away. When they later found it, it was standing atop Sullivan's lost mine.[58] Discovery of silver at Globe, atop a vast copper deposit, opened that region in 1874. Soon after, Tip Top and Peck Mines in the Bradshaw Mountains south of Prescott, along with McCracken and Signal Mines further west, became major producers.

The bonanza of Arizona silver strikes came in 1877, when a sourdough named Ed Schieffelin located his Tombstone claim in the barren and unpromising mountains of Cochise County. Twenty years earlier, the German prospector Frederick Brunckow had opened a mine nearby, but Apaches killed him before it made him wealthy. Tombstone had an unprecedented, though brief, productive period. During its five to six years of operation, silver ore valued at close to fifty million dollars was extracted and Tombstone became one of the most spectacular, colorful, and infamous camps in the west. Ed Schieffelin and his brother Al sold out to investors at a healthy profit in 1880.

Tombstone's bonanza days ended in 1888, when virtually all the mines in the district had to be abandoned because of a tremendous and uncontrollable flood of underground water below five hundred feet. By the time Tombstone's silver mines were abandoned, copper was becoming Arizona's most important natural resource. By 1870, commercial enterprises, financiers and miners alike were beginning to sense the potential of copper.

---

58. Marshall Trimble, *Arizona: A Calvalcade of History* (1990).

Ed Schieffelin, discoverer of the legendary Tombstone silver mines.
(PHOTO: MARSHALL TRIMBLE)

Thus there was growing incentive for the development of the many large high-grade copper ore bodies in Arizona. Also, the coming of the railroads to southern Arizona in the early 1880s was a tremendous boon to the developing copper industry. The copper industry and the freight revenues it generated likewise made it easier for the railroad builders to attract the capital to expand their facilities.

Rich copper deposits were discovered at Globe in 1874; and in the Black Range northeast of Prescott, a mountain of rich copper ore was located two years later. By 1886 the first copper concentrator in the state had been built by William Church at Joy's Camp (later Morenci)—a significant step forward for the copper industry.

Perhaps no single individual in Arizona contributed more to advancing the industrial operation of the mining business than Dr. James Douglas, a Canadian medical doctor turned mining engineer, who arrived in Arizona in 1880. He was sent there by the Phelps Dodge Company to survey ore deposits reported at Jerome, Morenci, and Bisbee. It was largely through his efforts that the Phelps Dodge Company grew to its great size, and he finally became president of the company. Earlier, Douglas and another medical doctor had developed a new process for extracting copper from difficult ore. For this discovery, he received broad recognition from the metal processing industry.

It would be impossible in the space of this book to mention all of the individual mining camps that sprang up throughout Arizona in the later half of the nineteenth century. There is much that has been written about this industry, and the histories of individual camps which can be obtained elsewhere: from the records in the offices of the various county recorders, records on file with the Arizona Department of Mineral Resources, records on file with the United States Bureau of Mines, and, of course, in the public libraries.

Ranching and Livestock

As far as is known, the first cattle imported to the New World were a few Andalusian heifers and a young bull brought to Mexico in 1521 by Gregorio de Villalobos. He acquired them from the island of Santo Domingo in the West Indies, where they had been bred from the original Spanish herds.[59] But it was the indefatigable Father Kino who gets the credit for introducing livestock to Arizona, where he not only introduced cattle, but goats, sheep, and horses as well. Throughout the eighteenth century, stock raising developed rapidly until it had become the most reliable source of income from the haciendas. Spanish herds expanded northward, laying the foundation of the cattle industry in

59. Edward H. Peplow, *History of Arizona* (1958).

the valleys and on the plains of present-day Arizona. We are told that even before the Mexican Revolution, stock raisers were petitioning Spanish authorities for government pasture lands; after the Revolution, they continued to seek grants from the Mexican government. By the 1830s, ranches were thriving as far north as Tucson. During those times it appears that the Arizona ranges were considerably different from what they are today, with plenty of grass and water to sustain large herds.

It is believed that William Kirkland became the first American to undertake ranching operations when he acquired the Canoa Ranch forty miles south of Tucson, soon after the Gadsden Purchase. William S. Oury of Tucson is believed to have been the next, when he bought a small herd of one hundred heifers and four bulls from a drover from Illinois on a drive through to California. In 1854, Pete Kitchen came to Arizona and stayed at the Canoa Ranch for a time before taking up his Potreto Ranch near Nogales about 1860. Due to the Civil War and the absence of troops in the territory, the livestock industry came to a virtual standstill except for the Kitchen Ranch.

Immediately after the return of Union troops, however, new attempts were made to restock the range. About 1866, Texans again turned their attention to western markets to dispose of the surplus stock that had piled up on their ranges during the Civil War. The 1870s marked the beginning of the era of what is known as the "big cow outfits." The demand for beef was growing, and the market at the military posts and the Indian reservations was a ready one. Apaches and other warlike tribes were the main and almost only detriment to ranching until the early 1880s, when the great bulk of them were gathered onto reservations.

The advent of the transcontinental railroads signaled a great land rush in the territory. Some forty million acres were available for grazing purposes. Some of it belonged to descendents of Spanish families through land grant title; ten million acres was the property of the Atlantic and Pacific Railroad, granted to it by the United States government as an inducement to build a railroad; and certain other lands were reserved for Indians. But that left a vast and seemingly limitless range on which cattlemen might settle and claim.

Bert Haskett writes, "The abundance of the grasses, the mildness of the climate and the general fitness of the country for the production of cattle in large numbers, served to encourage many adventurous spirits both throughout the United States and in foreign lands to try the cattle business in the new *El Dorado* of the Southwest where grass was free and law was lax. And so it was that every running stream and every living spring was settled upon; ranch homes were built and the adjoining ranges stocked with cattle brought in on foot and by rail from the north Mexican states and from the territories and states of the Union as far east as Maryland. Many of the newcomers were from Texas, the state that has produced more cattle than any area of equal size perhaps in the world. These men knew cattle and ranges and how to carry on. They liked the country, made their homes here, raised families, and contributed to the building of a new state."[60]

But the freewheeling days of the open range in much of Arizona drew to a close with the dawn of the twentieth century. Gone were the days when large ranchers enjoyed free and unregulated use of government land to graze their extensive herds of cattle. Outsiders began moving in with legal claims to small plots under the Homestead Law.

During the boom years large numbers of Easterners were lured to Arizona in search of wealth, setting off a population swell at the end of the nineteenth century: the territory's population had reached eighty-eight thousand by 1890; twenty years later, it had grown to the astounding figure of more than two hundred thousand.

Religion

Catholic missionaries contributed immensely to the early exploration and settlement of present-day southern Arizona. Had it not been for the work of Father Kino and his successors, it is likely that Arizona would have

---

60. Edward H. Peplow, "Early History of the Cattle Industry in Arizona," *Arizona Historical Review*, Vol. Vi, No 4, Oct. 1935. (Taken from Peplow, *History of Arizona*, 1958).

remained an unexplored wilderness for much longer. Throughout much of the eighteenth century and into the early part of the nineteenth, major missionary efforts were directed by the Jesuits and then the Franciscans toward the native population, as well as toward providing spiritual guidance for Spanish and Mexican settlers in the area.

In the aftermath of the Mexican Revolution, the expulsion of the Franciscans, and the subsequent Gadsden Purchase, attempts to institute organized religion in the territory encountered some obstacles. The territory seemed to be dedicated far more to bloodshed and violence, greed and lust than to concerns of the soul. In 1853, Santa Fe was made an Episcopal See of the Catholic Church and Arizona was included as part of the diocese. Father Machebeuf was dispatched to Tucson in 1859 to find there had been no resident priest in the Old Pueblo since the Franciscans were expelled more than thirty years earlier. Accordingly, Father Machebeuf assumed the post himself. We are told that he was particularly charmed by San Xavier, which was in a good state of preservation, and that he noted with satisfaction that the Indians there still retained a good deal of the religious training they had been given by the Franciscans.

In 1868, Arizona became a vicariate apostolic; the following year, Tucson was selected as an Episcopal See with Peter Bourgade as its first bishop. In 1880, the first Catholic parish, St. Mary's, was organized in Phoenix.

The Franciscans were given charge of St. Mary's, and they later established St. John's Mission for the Pima Indians southwest of the city. A Catholic parish, Sacred Heart, was established in 1878 in Prescott.

Next to Catholicism, the religion that has had the greatest effect upon Arizona's history is that of the Church of Jesus Christ of Latter-day Saints, the Mormons. Migrating south from Utah, the Mormons established communities throughout Arizona, settling along the Little Colorado River and on the Mogollon Rim. Farther south, they established Mesa on the Salt River, Safford on the Gila, and St. David on the San Pedro. The earliest appearance of Mormons on the Arizona scene is said to have been in 1846, when a party of their missionaries visited the Hopi villages. The Hopis, however, were as unreceptive to the Mormon teachings as they had been to all efforts to convert them from their own religion.

Mormons were one of the most successful groups to come to Arizona in search of opportunity, and to practice their religion and way of life in peace, including the Mormon tradition of polygamy. When the United States government moved to prohibit polygamy in Utah, the members who followed this way of life moved south to the Territory of Arizona. In the mid-1880s, however, there arose so much hostility toward the practice of polygamy in Arizona that many polygamous families migrated again, this time to Mexico. Many of them would return after the Mexican Revolution erupted in 1910.

Peplow states that it is much more difficult to chronicle the history of Protestant churches in Arizona. The first Protestant missionary to arrive is believed to have been a Presbyterian minister, who traveled to the Navajos in 1869. Nine years later, the first Presbyterian church was established in Phoenix. The first Methodist minister to hold services of that denomination in Arizona was Rev. J.L. Dyer, who arrived in 1868. In 1879 the Rev. George Adams established the first formal Methodist organization in the territory and became its superintendent. The American Bible Society sent James Skinner to Prescott as a non-denominational missionary in 1868. The first Baptist activity was that of J.C. Bristow, an unlicensed preacher who delivered the first Baptist sermon at Middle Verde, near Camp Verde, in 1875.

The Episcopal Church is said to have been the slowest of the Protestant Churches to take root in Arizona. It was not until the 1880s, when Rev. George Dunlop was made bishop of Mexico and Arizona, that congregations were formed in Tucson, Phoenix, and Tombstone. In the closing decades of the nineteenth century and the early years of the twentieth, other Protestant congregations were formed throughout the state.

Catholics made up about two-thirds of the church population of Arizona in 1906. Mormons ranked second with between ten and fifteen percent, with Presbyterians and Methodists each having about half as many members as the Mormons.

9 FROM TERRITORY STATUS TO STATEHOOD

"Arizonans impatiently endured the long period of territorial status from 1863 to 1912. During these years men of determined political ambition migrated to the growing territory ... while awaiting personal opportunities, they often voiced unwarranted criticism and exaggerated the faults of territorial officials appointed by the incumbent president in far-away Washington.

—Bert M. Fireman, *Arizona: Historic Land*

On February 24, 1863, President Lincoln signed the Organic Act that created Arizona as a separate territory from New Mexico. The first appointed territorial governor was a "lame duck" congressman from Ohio named John Gurley. He died before taking office and was replaced by another ex-congressman, John Goodwin of Maine. Among the officials accompanying Goodwin to take over administration of the new territory were Robert C. McCormick of New York (Secretary of the

Territory); Joseph P. Allyn of Connecticut, William F. Turner of Iowa, and William T. Howell of Michigan (appointed judges); Almon Gage of New York (District Attorney); Levi Bashford of Wisconsin (Surveyor General); Milton Duffield of New York (United States Marshal); and Charles D. Poston, (Superintendent of Indian Affairs).

Tucson was their original destination, as the Old Pueblo was the only community in Arizona that could actually claim to be a community. They were planning to establish the capital in Tucson, until they visited General Jim Carleton at Fort Union, New Mexico. Calling Tucson a den of Southern sympathizers, Carleton suggested that the capital be located in the hinterlands, at a site near Fort Wipple and the gold fields in the Bradshaw Mountains. The first capital of Arizona was established on the west side of Granite Creek, at a site that become known as Prescott, after the popular historian William Hickling Prescott.

Following the course set out in the Northwest Ordinance of 1787 for creating new territories, Governor Goodwin directed Marshal Duffield to conduct a census of the new area. Returns disclosed 4,573 settlers, including soldiers at military posts, a few blacks, and a handful of "tame" Indians.[61] The governor then designated voting districts and set July 18, 1864 as the date for the election of a legislature and of a delegate to Congress.

61. Bert M. Fireman, *Arizona: Historic Land* (1982).

John Goodwin did not remain governor for long. In September 1865, he was elected territorial delegate to Congress (the most coveted office in the territory, for it allowed the incumbent to reside in the nation's capital), and was off to Washington. Goodwin had defeated Charles Poston, the man who had worked so hard for separate territorial status. Shortly after his loss, Poston screamed "fraud" in an ad he placed in a New York newspaper. He then dropped out of the Arizona limelight for thirteen years, during which time he traveled to the Orient and embraced the ancient religion of Zoroastrianism. He returned to Arizona in 1877 as receiver for the Federal Land Office in Florence. While there, he began preparations to build a temple to the sun god on a hill near the Gila River, which he called Primrose Hill. Many years after his death, Poston's remains were returned to Florence and entombed on the hill, afterwards called Poston's Butte.

Arizona's first territorial legislature convened its first meeting at Prescott on September 26, 1864. Upon Goodwin's election to the delegate position, the office of governor fell to Richard McCormick. The person chosen as speaker of the lower house was a zealous frontier lawyer by the name of W. Claude Jones, who only two years earlier had denounced President Lincoln and urged the residents of the Gadsden Purchase to join the Confederacy. But the past Confederate sympathies of Speaker Jones and other southern members

189

was of little significance, as northerners far outnumbered southerners in the legislative body.[62]

The legislature was bicameral with an upper chamber called the Council and a lower chamber called the House. They met annually until 1871, after which point they convened every other year for sixty-day sessions. Three years after opening the first legislature at Prescott, Tucson secured enough votes to take the territorial capital to the Old Pueblo, where it would remain for ten years. It returned to Prescott in 1877 and remained there until 1889, when it was given a permanent location in a new community that was emerging in the Salt River Valley near the junction of the Salt and Gila Rivers, not far from Fort McDowell. It was given the name Phoenix for the mythical bird who miraculously arose from its burning ashes, reborn and radiant, just as the new town in the Salt River Valley emerged from the ashes of the once great Hohokam Indian culture.

Phoenix began as a modest farming community shortly after Fort McDowell was built in the 1860s. It was the area's second farming phase, the first having flourished from around 300 to 1400 A.D. when Hohokam Indians formed their canals and directed the water of the Salt River to fields of beans, squash, and corn. From their departure until 1868, few had occupied the area, except farther south where the Ackimoel O'odham and

---

62. Ibid.

Maricopa Indians farmed along the Gila River. The lack of a steady water supply hindered large-scale agricultural development before the turn of the century. To remedy the situation, the federal government constructed the Roosevelt Dam east of the town, and soon fields of cotton and groves of citrus were flourishing in the desert valley. Notwithstanding its past popularity as farm country, Phoenix really came into its own as a prosperous urban metropolis in the twentieth century. By the 1920s, it had grown to be the largest city in Arizona. Toward the later part of the century it—and its suburban communities of Scottsdale, Mesa, Glendale, Chandler, Tempe, and Peoria—had emerged into one of the nation's leading metropolitan areas.

Desperados and Justice

Much has been written about Arizona's lawlessness and gunplay during the territorial years, and its outlaws and ruffians have attracted the focus of many writers and moviemakers. However, the unsung heroes are those lawmen of Arizona who distinguished themselves by turning back a horde of misfits who might have otherwise succeeded in imposing their style of frontier justice on the law-abiding citizens of the territory.

Madeline F. Paré writes that Commodore Perry Owens, Sheriff of Apache County in 1887, was met with gunfire when he tried to serve a warrant on Andy

Cooper at Holbrook on a charge of stealing cattle. Cooper was a member of the Blevins family, which was involved in the Pleasant Valley vendetta between the Tewksburys and the Graams. Two of his half-brothers and a cowboy companion joined in the attack on the sheriff. But within a few minutes, Owens had killed three of his attackers and wounded a fourth, as Paré describes it, "in a remarkable exhibition of bravery and rifle marksmanship."

Robert Paul was a peace officer who became so familiar in territorial law enforcement that his death in 1901 was front-page news across the west. Described as a six-foot, six-inch, 240-lb. Irishman from Lowell, Massachusetts, Robert arrived in Arizona in 1878 to work for Wells Fargo. By the early 1880s, he was Sheriff of Pima County. His reputation for running down robbers became legendary. When bandits Dick Hart, Tom Johnson, and Larry Sheehan headed into Mexico after holding up the Southern Pacific train at Stein's Pass, Robert pursued them. With the help of Mexican soldiers, he then tracked them to a ranch house in Chihuahua, where a running battle followed that killed the bandits. Robert Paul received national acclaim, and three years later President Harrison named him United States Marshal—a position he held until 1893.

One of the most respected sheriffs to wear the badge in Arizona was Carl Hayden, the state's first and longest serving member of Congress. As Sheriff of Maricopa County, Carl Hayden had an enviable record for arresting criminals and enforcing the law, yet he never once wore a revolver or carried a rifle.

Violent duels between miners and gamblers, lawmen and rustlers were commonplace and, in its day, there was no more notorious place in Arizona than Tombstone. Here, saloons, gambling houses, and a variety of other businesses were crammed into an area half a mile long and a few blocks wide. Fortune hunters, lured by Ed Schieffelin's fabulous silver discovery in 1877, flooded in by the thousands. One author described it as among the last of the big boon towns where gamblers, desperadoes, and adventurers had a "last chance" to subscribe to lawlessness before decent law abiding people succeeded in reclaiming the area.

Some historians attribute the lawlessness of the period to the conditions of the nation in the aftermath of the Civil War. Many veterans, having experienced the horrors of war, arrived home to find their homes and communities devastated, fortunes lost, and families uprooted or separated. For many of them, the West offered a fresh start with which new dreams might be fulfilled; for others, it was an opportunity to flout the law.

During the 1880s, Tombstone became Arizona's, and for that matter the West's, most notorious and violent boomtown. Its population rocketed to a peak of fifteen thousand inhabitants in 1883; by 1888, more than thirty million dollars worth of gold and silver had been extracted from its mines. The area had become so

Johnny Behan, first sheriff of Cochise County. (PHOTO: MARSHALL TRIMBLE)

populous that a separate county, Cochise, was carved from the eastern part of Pima. Tombstone was made the county seat, and a "political hack" named Johnny Behan (according to some historians, more interested in getting wealthy than enforcing the law in the county) was appointed sheriff.

The stories of Tombstone's violent years are abundant. Many of them, however, relate to a single dramatic episode, where an encounter between two groups of trigger-happy men led to a shootout at Tombstone's O.K. Corral (more likely the corner of Freemont and Third streets). There, on October 26, 1881, the Earp gang—City Marshal, Virgil W. Earp; his younger brothers and deputies, Wyatt and Morgan; and their friend, John H. "Doc" Holliday—battled the Clanton "cowboys": Ike and Billy Clanton,

Tom and Frank McLaury, and Billy Claiborne. The gunfight grew out of a long and bitter struggle for power in Cochise County. The Earp brothers were the enforcers for the Citizens' Safety Committee, while the Clanton "cowboys" rustled cattle under the guise of honest ranchers.

Wyatt Earp, who served as a Wells Fargo undercover agent, Pima County deputy sheriff, and U.S. deputy marshal.

On that fateful occasion, the Clanton gang was preparing to leave town, having retrieved their guns (which the law required them to turn in upon entering the town) and readying to mount their horses, when the Earps tried to arrest them. Accounts differ as to which party began the shooting, but in fifteen seconds it was finished. Within this short time, the McLaury brothers and Billy Clanton were dead, and Morgan and Virgil Earp wounded. In its wake, the Earps were charged with murder, but managed to stay out of jail awaiting a trial that was never held.

Friends of the dead trio sneaked back into Tombstone by night to settle accounts. A hidden assailant sprayed Virgil with a shotgun blast, permanently crippling his arm. Morgan was shot dead while playing a game of pool. After a wild foray into the mountains in which they killed one or more friends of the Clantons, and after shooting down another in the Tucson railroad yard, the remaining Earps fled from Arizona and successfully avoided extradition from Colorado.

Despite their reputed prowess as law enforcement officers, the Earp brothers left Tombstone in a state of lawlessness—a condition that they had failed to diminish, and may have even heightened. This fact led President Chester A. Arthur to issue a proclamation that condemned conditions in the territory and threatened military action if they continued. But the intervention of the federal government was not necessary; the citizens of the county called upon one of their most prominent cattlemen, John H. Slaughter, to become sheriff. Slaughter conducted a ruthless and effective assault upon the desperadoes, finally driving them out of the county.

Tombstone's final act of real-life Wild West theater was staged on November 16, 1900, when Texas-born brothers Thomas and William Halderman were publicly hanged for the murder of two lawmen. The violence had erupted one year earlier, when rancher Buck

Smith swore out a warrant accusing the two brothers of shooting some of his cattle. The Haldermans were charged with gunning down the lawmen as they attempted to serve the warrant. A lengthy trial ensued at which defense lawyers amassed evidence that, according to some writers, should have set the brothers free. However, none of it swayed the jury. While the brothers were awaiting execution, an incident occurred that should have brought them public sympathy. Three train robbers broke out of the Tombstone jail, shot a deputy, and then opened the cell doors to allow the other prisoners to flee. But instead of fleeing with the rest of the prisoners, the Haldermans stayed and tended to the deputy's wounds. Ungratefully, the local *Prospector* wrote that it was "a shrewd attempt to divert public sympathy in their favor."

Among the law-abiding citizens of Tombstone was a little Irish lady named Nellie Cashman, who is remembered as one of the most remarkable and benevolent persons to have lived among Tombstone's lawless and rough-hewn characters. For most of fifty adventurous years, she trekked between mining camps from Mexico to Alaska and was already a legend among the sourdoughs of the West and Northwest by the time she joined in the silver rush to Tombstone in 1880. Nellie staked claims, led mining expeditions, and operated restaurants and boarding houses for miners from Tombstone to the Yukon. She was a legend in her own time for her virtuous deeds. During a scurvy outbreak

Nellie Cashman, "Angel of the Mining Camp." A prospector, humanitarian, and entrepreneur, her wanderlust took her from Mexico to the Yukon.

among snowbound miners of Cassiar, British Columbia in 1877, she arranged, at her own expense, to have a shipment of vegetables sent into the camp to aid the stricken "sourdoughs." For this charitable act, she became affectionately known as the "Angel of the Miners."

During her time in Tombstone, Nellie ran a boarding house. Compassionate and generous to a fault, Nellie never refused to lend a hand to the ill-fated. On one occasion in Tombstone, she smuggled a visiting mine superintendent out of town in her buggy, after she learned that he was about to be kidnapped and lynched by some enraged miners. When five desperados were about to be hanged at the county courthouse for their part in the "Bisbee Massacre," a get-rich-quick operator erected a grandstand so that the curious, for a fee, could view the hangings over the wall. The condemned men appealed to Nellie to prevent their execution from becoming a public exhibition, and an indignant Nellie rounded up a few friends to demolish the structure the night before the hanging. Nellie was also known for her fund-raising talent. In 1882, she raised the funds to build Tombstone's Catholic Church, and is believed to have put up much of the money herself.

The Road to Statehood

Throughout its forty-nine years as a territory, Arizona worked hard at becoming a full-fledged state in the Union. It was reasoned that Arizona's citizens had more right to control their affairs than had a collection of officials appointed by Washington. In 1889, Governor C. Meyer Zulick summed up the feelings of most Arizonans on the question of statehood when he declared, "A territorial government, depriving, as it does, the citizen of full participation in the government under which he lives, is repugnant to the enlightenment sense of the American people, and there is no question but that our progress would be more rapid and our prosperity would be quickened if these disabilities were removed."[63]

---

63. Edward H. Peplow, *History of Arizona* (1958).

There were many advocates of statehood at work throughout the 1880s and 1890s. But the first real attempt to draft a state constitution was in 1891, when a non-partisan constitutional convention convened in Phoenix. Among the items placed in the constitution were a provision for the establishment of silver as legal currency for the payment of state debts and the declaration that all rivers were state property. While these and other provisions were understandably important for many Arizonans, they were considered preposterous by many Easterners, so Congress lost no time in rejecting the constitution. The issue of free silver (opposed by politicos favoring the gold standard) was a highly charged political topic in Washington.

A bill providing for the free and unlimited coinage of silver was rejected by the House in June of 1889. Had it passed, it might have meant the free silver forces were strong enough to expedite statehood for Arizona. Instead, the Sherman Silver Purchase Act passed, which required the government to buy certain quantities of silver in order to stabilize its price. Four years later, a national financial panic forced the repeal of the Sherman Act, and the country moved from a bi-metal standard to the gold standard. The result was an immediate and disastrous drop in the price of silver, which resulted in the closure of many mines throughout Arizona and large-scale unemployment among the miners.

Late in 1893, another Phoenix convention convened and tried to approach Congress more artfully with a petition for statehood. It was personally taken to Washington by Governor Nathan Murphy and, although rejected, appears to have paved the way for the 1894 passage of the Enabling Act by the House of Representatives. This act sanctioned the organization of the State of Arizona.

In the meantime, Arizona's population was growing rapidly. The census of 1870 showed Arizona with a population of 9,658; the 1880 census recorded 40,440 inhabitants—a phenomenal increase of almost four hundred percent. By 1900 the population had increased another fifty percent, and yet another sixty percent by 1910. The railroads were making it much easier for the more adventuresome would-be settlers to come to Arizona and, by the same token, the railroads were proving a great boon to the territory's economy. The burgeoning population and the growing economy would inevitably encourage recognition by Washington of the territory's demands for autonomy.

The first really solid encouragement came in the Republican Party platform of 1900, which included a plank in favor of the early admission to statehood for Arizona, New Mexico, and Oklahoma. Despite a visit to Arizona by President McKinley in 1901, no action came about. McKinley made only vague promises to aid in the movement for statehood. However, optimism was renewed the following year, during the first administration of President Theodore Roosevelt, many of whose Rough Riders of the Cuban Invasion had been recruited in Arizona.

Forces in Congress remained stubbornly opposed. Spokesman and leader of this opposition was Senator Albert J. Beveridge of Indiana. Returning from a visit to Arizona with other members of the Senate Sub-Committee on Statehood, he sarcastically remarked, "Arizona is a mining camp, and the bill admitting her is gerrymandered so shamefully that if the Republicans were to carry the State by ten thousand, she would still send two Democratic senators to Washington."[64] Shortly thereafter, proponents of statehood sent a committee headed by William Randolph Hearst, and the findings of this group were as favorable as Beveridge's were unfavorable.

Arizona found itself facing a much more serious setback in 1904, when an amendment was attached to the statehood bill calling for New Mexico and Arizona to be admitted to the Union as one state. As anticipated, the reaction against the proposed jointure was swift and forceful. Arizonans united into a cohesive and effective fighting force, organizing the Anti-Joint Statehood League. The Arizona Legislature convened in January 1905 and passed a concurrent resolution of protest that, in part, read: "We insist that such [joint statehood] is without precedent in American History. It threatens to fasten upon us a government that would be neither of,

---

64. Ibid.

by, nor for the people of Arizona. It would be a government without the consent of the governed. It humiliates our pride, violates our tradition and would subject us to the domination of another commonwealth of different traditions, customs and aspirations . . ."

Arizona's resoluteness garnered the support of some powerful senators who persuaded the Senate to amend the joint statehood bill, and to allow the two territories to express their own wishes in regard to union. The House rejected the Senate amendment, however, and forced the matter into abeyance for a year. In 1906 the situation reversed itself; the House quickly passed the amended bill, but the Senate battle was renewed with Senator Beveridge leading the fight for jointure. A compromise "whereby the Territories (Arizona and New Mexico) might individually give expression to their preferences by means of the ballot" moved the bill out of the Senate, and the House quickly approved its passage.

A vote in each territory on the question in November 1906 showed that Arizona was very definitely opposed, with 16,265 against and only 3,141 for joint statehood. The New Mexico count had 26,195 for union and 14,735 against. Arizona's steadfastness began to reap dividends when both major political parties included planks in their 1908 platforms that favored separate statehood for both Arizona and New Mexico. Two years later, the victorious Republicans kept their promise and passed a bill through Congress that enabled Arizona to hold elections for members of a constitutional convention. Once selected, the delegated would then draw up the constitution of Arizona as a separate state. President Taft hastily approved the measure, and the election of delegates to the constitutional convention ensued.

Election results confirmed an overwhelming victory for the Democratic Party, forty-one of the fifty-two delegates elected being Democrats. In 1911 the convention drafted a constitution that was ratified by Arizonans by a vote of almost four to one. The Constitution was duly submitted to Congress for approval and, after amending the recall provision to exclude the judiciary, it finally passed. With all the preparatory work concluded, President Taft signed the proclamation admitting Arizona to the Union at 10:00 a.m. on February 14, 1912.

From the time it was first visited by Europeans, it had taken Arizona three hundred years to finally achieve the status of a distinct political entity. During its long career, writes historian Edward H. Peplow, Jr., it had been at various times a mysterious wilderness concealing the fabulous Seven Golden Cities of Cibola; a forgotten and neglected wilderness; a rich field of missionary activity; the unwanted and unprotected step-child of Spanish Mexico; the forgotten outpost of Mexico; the alluring treasure house where mountain men surreptitiously sought fortunes in fur and gold; the unwanted appendage of New Mexico; the sudden mecca of miners and prospectors; the blood-stained battleground of the Apache Wars; first the territory of the Confederacy and then, at last, a separate territory of the United States; the wondrously rich haven of cattlemen, sheepmen, and miners; again a blood-stained battlefield in the wars between stockmen and rustlers, cattlemen and sheepmen, law-officers and outlaws, and Mexican revolutionists and American citizens; the target of master swindlers, corporate greed, and political opportunists; and finally the haven for the home seeker, the health seeker and the seeker after beauty and a new and better way of life.

BEYOND STATEHOOD

Six descendents of nineteenth-century Arizona pioneers came to national prominence in the second half of the twentieth century. They were Carl Hayden, Barry Goldwater, brothers Stewart and Morris Udall, Sandra Day O'Connor, and Bruce Babbitt, and they all made important contributions to their state and their nation.

Full-fledged statehood finally came to fulfillment on February 14, 1912, with the formal proclamation signed by President William Howard Taft that admitted Arizona as the forty-eighth, or last of the contiguous states. The railroads completed in the late 1870s and early 1880s made it much easier for the more adventuresome would-be settlers to move to the territory and acquire land. As more newcomers arrived, the population expanded and demands for autonomy eventually heightened. In the interlude, Arizona attracted its

James Addison Reavis, the self-styled "Baron of Arizona."

share of sinister characters, among them outlaws, manipulators, and con men.

James Addison Reavis, who died in Denver in 1914, was the perpetrator of one of the most bizarre swindle attempts in nineteenth-century Arizona. Reavis, a one-time street-car conductor from Missouri and the self-styled "Baron of Arizona," was one of the slickest con men of his time, claiming title to a Spanish land grant encompassing 3,750 square miles of some of the most desirable land in Arizona in the heart of Pimeria Alta.

Essentially, his story was that King Fernando VI of Spain had conferred upon Miguel Peralta de Cordova, by credula of December 20, 1748, the title of Baron de los Colorados in reward for his services to the crown. Peralta died in 1788 and his estate, and presumably his title, passed to his son Miguel Peralta II. This second Baron of the Colorados died in 1864, and the claim to the title supposedly passed to an American relative, George M. Willing, Jr. Willing died mysteriously in Prescott in 1874, where he had gone to file the claim. Nothing more was heard of the claim until March 27, 1883, when Reavis showed up at the surveyor-general's office in Tucson with a handful of old, stained, and torn Spanish documents to register his claim to the Peralta Land Grant. As the authenticity of the claim was not then in question, Reavis title superceded all other titles within the area of the Peralta Land Grant by virtue of the 1848 Treaty of Guadalupe Hidalgo, in which the United States had pledged to recognize all former land grants and to hold such claims inviolable.

Suffice to say Reavis' amazing and elaborate hoax succeeded until it was exposed in the early 1890s. In the meantime, he established the Casa Grande Land Improvement Company at Arizola. Influential eastern investors and politicians became part of the operation. Supposedly, John W. Mackay, of Comstock Lode wealth and fame, provided substantial favors to Reavis. Tributes were regularly collected from settlers and from the Southern Pacific Railroad for crossing his purported property. Reavis and his family lived in elegant style, maintaining imposing homes in Chicago, Washington, and Chihuahua City, Mexico.

The circumstances whereby Reavis had received the original Spanish documents continued to raise suspicions, until an Arizona printer had occasion to examine them and, to his disbelief, detected they had been printed from type that he had designed. It was later proved that the paper on which they were printed was not more than twenty years old and, when held up to the light, showed the unmistakable watermark of a paper mill near Appleton, Wisconsin. In a much-publicized hearing before a United States Court of Private Land Claims in Santa Fe in 1895, the Peralta Grant was finally invalidated. Charges of fraud were then filed against Reavis. In 1896, the self-styled "Baron of Arizona" was sentenced to two years in a federal penitentiary.

Labor Strife and the Bisbee Deportation

For close to thirty years before the first decade of the twentieth century, mining companies relied on workers who were skillful at extracting ore with little supervision. Mining methods began to change after 1900, as modern machinery replaced old equipment, and management procedures took on a more sophisticated appearance. These changes brought about new relationships, as miners became more subordinate in their work environment, with less leverage to bargain for wages and working conditions. In response, miners joined unions in large numbers and as the unions became more powerful, the mining companies' aversion to them grew.

When the copper miners at Bisbee attempted to form a union in 1906, the mine managers fired and black-listed hundreds who supported the unionization effort. Another decade would pass before such organization was attempted again. In the meantime, the social philosophy of the Progressive Era had become very influential in Arizona politics, and unions were playing a conspicuous role where the worker was concerned.

In the fall of 1910, forty-one Democratic and eleven Republican delegates gathered in Phoenix to draft Arizona's constitution. There was much concern about the role of big corporations and the safety and welfare of their employees. Labor unions, with strong support from the Democratic delegates, pushed and got pro-labor provisions like regulation of child labor, an eight-hour day for public employees, and compensation rights for workers in dangerous jobs. Labor was not as successful in other demands: union workers' right to strike was dismissed, as was a clause that would have denied judges the power to issue injunctions against strikers.

In the early years of the century, union organizational efforts centered on enlisting workers who were mainly of European background. Many unions denied membership to Mexican Americans, Mexican immigrants, and blacks, and went as far as to have a provision written into the state constitution that anyone who could not "speak the English language" be prohibited from working in "underground or other hazardous occupations"—that is, in the mines or on the railroads (the best paying jobs in the territory). Discriminatory measures against Mexican workers undercut labor union efforts to build strong and effective worker organizations in the mining towns of the Southwest. World War I and its great demand for copper rescued the union movement, when the federal government prohibited the mine operators from firing workers who had gone out on strike in 1917.

Their hands tied, mine operators fanned the fires of popular fears with a constant flow of patriotic, anti-strike propaganda. Led by Walter Douglas of Phelps Dodge, they mounted a counteroffensive against the unions, charging German influence behind the union movement and calling upon the individual communities to rise up and drive out this disruptive element. The *Bisbee Daily Review*, the company-controlled newspaper, kept up a steady flow of anti-unionism, while company officials and the county sheriff made plans to deport the strikers. The deportation process was initiated on the morning of July 12, 1917, when two thousand vigilantes, deputized by Sheriff Henry Wheeler of Cochise County, burst into homes and boardinghouses and arrested 1,986 strikers. Without due process, the strikers were marched by the vigilantes to a nearby ballpark, and one-by-one were offered the choice of returning to work or being deported. Eight hundred miners agreed to go back to work; 1,186 refused and were immediately loaded onto railroad boxcars and shipped to Hermanas, New Mexico, where they were dropped off in the middle of the desert without food or water.

Appalled by the cruelty inflicted upon the strikers, President Wilson appointed a federal commission to investigate and, early the next year, the federal government brought charges against Cochise County officials and Phelps Dodge executives, including Sheriff Wheeler and Walter Douglas, for conspiracy and kidnapping. All of the individuals charged were finally acquitted, after their lawyers successfully convinced the United States Supreme Court that their clients hadn't broken any existing federal law.

Politics and Political Leaders

Arizona has enjoyed a remarkably unruffled political existence, considering its hectic and protracted struggle in achieving statehood. The first Arizona State Legislature gave women the right to vote, eight years before suffrage was obtained nationally. Two years later, in 1914, Rachel Allen Berry was elected to the State House and Frances Willard to the State Senate, making them the first women in the nation to serve in a state legislature. It was not until 1948, however, that Indians were the given the right to vote. The delay was due to confusion over their status—whether they were United States citizens or residents of a foreign nation within the borders of the United States.

In the first state election, Democrat George W.P. Hunt beat Republican J.F. Cleveland for the governorship. Democrats Henry F. Ashurst and Marcus A. Smith were elected the first United States senators, and Democrat Carl Hayden the first Arizona representative in Congress. Little more than a month after the first state officials were inaugurated, the First State Legislature assembled in Phoenix to enact several important pieces of legislation, including the creation of the office of attorney general and adoption of a code for the regulation of corporations. Historian Edward H. Peplow notes that it was at this session the young state asserted its right to self-determination by passing the provision for the recall of judges, which originally had been struck from its constitution by President Taft and Congress.

Politics in Arizona was the bailiwick of the Democratic Party throughout the territorial and statehood years until after World War II. At times some gubernatorial races were tight as, for example, the 1916 race between Democratic incumbent Hunt and Republican challenger Campbell. Tom Campbell was the winner by a mere thirty votes, and he and the other state officials were sworn in on January 1, 1917. In the meantime, Hunt demanded a recount, and the result showed him to be the winner by forty-three votes. He then went to court, but Judge Rawghlie Clement Stanford (a fellow Democrat and later governor) ruled against him.

Governor George W.P. Hunt, territorial legislator, president of the constitutional convention on statehood, and first governor of the State of Arizona.

Mark Smith was a Tombstone lawyer during the heyday of the silver camp. In 1912, he was elected as one of the first two senators from the new state of Arizona.

Carl Hayden, descendant of a pioneer family, was Arizona's first and longest-serving representative in Congress.

He appealed the decision to the State Supreme Court, where Hunt's claim to the governorship was affirmed on the basis of the re-count. Tom Campbell had served in office eleven months, before Hunt came in officially to finish the term. Campbell finally won the governorship in 1918, beating the Democratic standard-bearer, Fred Colter, by fewer than four hundred votes; in 1920, he rode a national Republican landslide to his first comfortable victory.

Throughout the Depression years, the Democratic Party retained almost complete control of state politics. However, the great increase in Arizona's population during the war years signaled a shift to the Republican side in the 1946 election, when Republican candidate Bruce Brockett amassed the largest number of votes by a Republican gubernatorial candidate in many years. Even more indicative of the changing political atmosphere was the passage of the "right-to-work" referendum in 1946. Generally thought of as more Republican than Democratic in concept, the right-to-work law placed certain restrictions on the powers and activities of labor unions and prohibited the denial of a job to a person because of membership or lack of membership in a union. It was passed by 61,875 votes to 49,557. The issue was a major point of controversy in the campaign, and remains a recurrent point of controversy to this day.

As Arizona's communities and economy transformed themselves, so did the politics of the state.

With the influx of newcomers, Arizona's progressive legacy and the Democratic majority gave way to a solid, conservative group of voters and an equally resolute Republican party. The 1950 campaign was the turning point in Arizona politics, ending a Democratic reign that had been interrupted only twice in its thirty-eight years of statehood. The election of 1952 witnessed a distinct shift when Arizonans, for the first time in more than twenty years, voted for Republican presidential candidate Dwight D. Eisenhower. At the same time, they gave Republican Howard Pyle an overwhelming vote for governor over his Democratic opponent, Joe Haldiman. Senator Ernest W. McFarland, who had been Democratic Majority Leader in the Senate, was voted out; his spot was captured by a young Arizona businessman and heir of one of Arizona's oldest pioneer mercantile families, Barry Goldwater. Twelve years later, Goldwater would be the Republican standard-bearer in the race for United States President.

McFarland returned to the political arena in 1954 and beat Howard Pyle for the governorship; at the same time, he helped the state Democrats recover a few of the seats lost in the Eisenhower landslide. After two terms as governor, he made an unsuccessful attempt to take back his former senate seat from Goldwater. MacFarland was later elected to the Arizona Supreme Court. After losing the race for president in 1964, Barry Goldwater was elected to the Senate to fill the position vacated by the retiring Carl Hayden.

By the early 1980s, supporters of the New Right had displaced the older conservative elite led by politicians such as Barry Goldwater. The New Right, more a coalition than a movement, drew much of its support from religious conservatives such as evangelical Protestants, conservative Catholics, and orthodox Jews who hoped to direct government activism into moral reforms, such as support for prayer in public schools and for making abortion illegal. Arizonans and other Americans found the New Right's opposition to "big government" particularly inviting, as they became exposed to one political scandal after another. Two governors—Evan Mecham in 1988 and Fife Symington in 1997—were removed from office. An investigation into corruption in the state assembly in 1991 resulted in the bribery conviction of eighteen individuals, including state senators, house representatives, lobbyists, and Democratic Party officials.

Among Arizonans prominent on the national stage throughout the twentieth century were brothers Stewart and Morris Udall. Stewart served in the Kennedy Administration as Secretary of the Interior. Morris daringly challenged John McCormack for the House leadership position in 1969—the first contested election for nomination to the leadership since 1923. His challenge was unsuccessful, losing by a vote of 178 to 58. Congressman John Rhodes was elected Minority Leader by his Republican colleagues in 1973. Senator Ernest

McFarland served as Majority Leader of the Senate. Bruce Babbitt served as Secretary of the Interior in the Clinton Administration.

Arizonans William Rehnquist and Sandra Day O'Connor serve on the United States Supreme Court—O'Connor being the first woman to achieve this distinction. Rose Mofford, the daughter of Austrian immigrants and a native of Globe, became Arizona's first woman governor in 1988. Recently, Senator John McCain, a rising star in national politics, made an unsuccessful bid to be the Republican nominee for President.

Bruce Babbitt served as Arizona's governor from 1978–1987. During the Clinton administration, he served as Secretary of the Interior.

When Arizonan Sandra Day O'Connor was appointed to the Supreme Court by President Reagan in 1981, she made history as the first woman to serve on that august body.

Lieutenant Commander John McCain is greeted by President Nixon at a State Department reception for former prisoners of war. In 2000, McCain made an unsuccessful run for the Republican presidential nomination.

Growth and Prosperity

As Arizona prepares to celebrate its centennial as a state in 2012, one can only marvel at the dramatic changes that have taken place and at the obstacles that were overcome to make this parched land habitable and flourishing. What was a sparsely populated agrarian land in 1912, with mining and ranching as its chief enterprises, has become a fast-growing urban region with dense areas of population, primarily engaged in high-tech and service industries. This growth and prosperity might not have occurred without a dependable water supply—for Arizonans' the most precious of commodities. Securing a reliable water supply meant the building of dams, canals, pumps, and treatment plants to make this dry land a desert oasis.

Passage of the National Reclamation Act in 1902 relieved the money scarcity that had hampered pioneer farmers from fully harnessing available water resources. It provided for the necessary support to raise the enormous capital needed for construction of major aqueducts and storage dams, such as the huge Theodore Roosevelt Dam on the Salt River, completed in 1911 at a cost of ten million dollars. Started as an agrarian dream to irrigate fields of cotton, citrus, and vegetables, the Salt River project transformed metropolitan Phoenix into the largest urban city in the state by the middle of the twentieth century. Over the next few years, several smaller dams were built on the Salt to

Tonto Cliff Dwellings near Roosevelt Dam.

further strengthen irrigation throughout the Salt River Valley. The Coolidge Dam, completed in 1930, was a boon to farmers along the Gila River.

During the early twentieth century, new enterprises such as cotton farming joined established industries like ranching and copper mining to dominate the Southwestern economy. Tourism became an important factor; the state was a popular destination for many Americans with an affinity for frontier life, spectacular scenery, and plentiful sunshine. Hotels and resorts, dude ranches, restaurants, and other businesses patronized by tourists flourished.

The Great Depression was less severe in Arizona than in most other areas of the country. Nevertheless, the depression's financial shock waves hit Arizonans at every level of society. Workers and employers alike struggled to make ends meet as prices for copper, beef, cotton, and other agricultural products plummeted. Some mines closed down completely, while others drastically reduced operations. Between 1932 and 1936, Arizona's population decreased by some fifty thousand, as many packed their belongings and moved out of the state to seek work elsewhere.

World War II had a dramatic impact on Arizona's economy. The states raw materials—copper, livestock, cotton, and food crops—were once again in demand. Many war industries set up operations in the state, and Tucson and Phoenix quickly became centers for technological manufacturing. However, the shift created by

World War II and the post-war boom did not happen in a void. New Deal programs administered by the Works Progress Administration and the Civilian Conservation Corps had already put into place much of the infrastructure that made it possible for the boom to take place. Between 1940 and 1950, Arizona's population burgeoned by 250,000 to 750,000. The war was over in 1945, but the amazing growth and change that the wartime economy brought to Arizona had only just started.

After years of political maneuvering and litigation, construction commenced on the massive Central Arizona Project in the early 1970s. Through a system of pumps, water is carried into central Arizona via 190 miles of aqueduct to Phoenix and another 140 miles to Tucson, supplementing existing water resources for lands, cities, and towns dependent on underground water tables. These water-harnessing projects have facilitated Arizona's evolvement from desert to agriculture to urban development. Every phase of the state's development has depended, and will continue to depend, upon an adequate supply of water. With water, Arizona shifted from a frontier land to an urban society formed by city life and city industries.

Contemporary Arizona is a land of contradictions. It has been described by some as a land of contrasts, by others as a land of extremes, and by yet others as a land of enchantment and exceptional beauty. Few have described this more convincingly than native son Marshall Trimble, who characterizes Arizona as bringing together the romance of the Wild West with the challenge of space-age technology: where, in the foothills surrounding the flourishing modern cities of Phoenix and Tucson, one can still watch hard-riding cowboys lasso and brand cattle in much the same fashion as their great-grandfathers did a century or so ago; and where in the pastel-hued mesas, sand-gray deserts and salmon-colored canyons, Native Americans cling to a cultural lifestyle that has been handed down for generations.

TIMELINE OF CONCURRENT EVENTS

10000–500 B.C.	Cochise culture flourishes in southeastern Arizona.
8000–3000 B.C.	Chiricahua phase of the Cochise culture
5000–300 B.C.	San Pedro phase of the Cochise culture.
500 B.C.	Beginning of the Hohokam culture in Arizona.
200–500 A.D.	Basketmaker period of the Anasazi culture.
500–700 A.D.	Adjusted Basketmaker period of the Anasazi culture.
600–900 A.D.	Colonial period of the Hohokam culture.
700–1050 A.D.	Unfolding Pueblo period.
900–1200 A.D.	Sedentary period of the Hohokam culture in Arizona.
1000–1300 A.D.	Navajos and Apaches arrive in Arizona.

1050–1300 A.D.	The Great Pueblo period.
1100–1150 A.D.	Hopis move into their mesa-top dwellings.
1200 A.D.	Disappearance of the Mimbres people.
1200–1400 A.D.	Classic period of Hohokam culture.
1276–1299 A.D.	Period of great drought.
1300 A.D.	Casa Grande is built near Gila River.
1300–1700 A.D.	Next Pueblo period.
1400–1450 A.D.	Hohokams disappear.
1492 A.D.	Columbus discovers the New World.
1493 A.D.	Pope Alexander VI grants all lands discovered in Western Hemisphere to the Spanish monarchy.
1493 A.D.	Columbus returns to New World and brings twelve missionaries under Benedictine monk, Bernardo Buil.
1519 A.D.	Cortes invades Mexico.
1520 A.D.	Montezuma killed by his own people.
1521 A.D.	Cortes captures Mexico City and executes Emperor Cuauhtemoc.
1528 A.D.	Narvaez lands in Florida in April. Later in the year, his party is shipwrecked. De Vaca, Maldanado, Dorantes, and Esteban survive and begin their journey of seven and a half years.

1536 A.D.	De Vaca and his party reach Mexico City.
1539 A.D.	Fray Marcos de Niza and Esteban lead party northward from Culiacan and penetrate Arizona in search for the Seven Golden Cities of Cibola.
1540 A.D.	Francisco Vasquez de Coronado leads an expedition north and captures a Zuni Indian pueblo at Hawikuh in western New Mexico, believing it to be one of the legendary wealthy Seven Golden Cities of Cibola.
1540 A.D.	Don Garcia Lopez de Cardenas leads a westward expedition from Hawikuh to discover the Grand Canyon.
1582 A.D.	Antonio de Espejo leads expedition into Arizona.
1598 A.D.	Juan de Onate leads party of colonists to San Juan (New Mexico) to establish the first European settlement in the northern regions of New Spain.
1609 A.D.	Santa Fe, New Mexico founded.
1613 A.D.	Jesuits' first mission in New Spain established on Rio Mayo in present-day Sonora. By 1644, Jesuit

	missions established in thirty-five locations in present-day Sonora.
1675 A.D.	By this date, Franciscans have established missions in Hopiland.
1680 A.D.	Great Pueblo Indians uprising.
1687 A.D.	Padre Eusebio Francisco Kino establishes his first mission: Nuestra Senora de los Dolores in Sonora.
1694 A.D.	Padre Kino explores Santa Cruz and Gila Valleys and visits Casa Grande ruins.
1700 A.D.	Padre Kino lays original foundation of San Xavior del Bac.
1711 A.D.	Padre Kino dies at mission of Santa Maria Magdalena.
1736 A.D.	Padres Ingnacio Keller and Jacob Sedelmayer enter Arizona to continue extension of Padre Kino's work.
1751 A.D.	Pima Indians drive out missionaries from San Xavior del Bac and San Gabriel de Guevavi.
1752 A.D.	Presidio established at village of Tubac on the Santa Cruz River. First white settlement in Arizona.

1767 A.D.	Charles III of Spain bans Jesuits from Spanish dominions, including Arizona.
1768 A.D.	San Xavier del Bac is taken over by Franciscan Fray Francisco Garcés.
1775 A.D	Don Hugo O'Conor moves presidio from Tubac to Tucson, establishing the first white community in the Old Pueblo.
1775 A.D.	Bautista de Anza leaves Tubac to found presidio of San Francisco.
1776 A.D.	Fray Garcés explores northern Arizona.
1781 A.D.	Yuma Indians massacre Spanish settlers, including Fray Garcés. Closes Anza route to California.
1785 A.D.	Padre Carillo begins building of great church at San Xavier del Bac.
1810–21 A.D.	Period of great internal unrest in Mexico, climaxing in the independence of Mexico from Spain.
1821–1848 A.D.	All of Arizona part of the Republic of Mexico.
1824 A.D.	Abandonment of the Tumacacori Misson.

1824 A.D.	Sylvester and James O. Pattie, Bill Williams, and Kit Carson head into northern Arizona.
1827 A.D.	Abandonment of San Xavier Mission.
1830 A.D.	Pauline Weaver enters Arizona. Two years later, he views ruin on Casa Grande.
1834 A.D.	Mission properties are escheated to the Mexican state.
1837 A.D.	The *Junta* of Chihuahua promulgates the infamous "Proyecto de Guerra," offering bounties on Apache scalps.
	Massacre of Juan Jose and his band at Santa Rita, which incited Mangas Coloradas to launch a violent and protracted war against the Mexicans.
1845 A.D.	Texas becomes the twenty-eighth state. President Polk sends emissary to Mexico with offer to buy land west of Texas, including Arizona.
1846 A.D.	United States declares war against Mexico. Col. Stephen Watts Kearny enters Santa Fe and proclaims civil government in New Mexico.
1846 A.D.	Mormon battalion takes possession of Tucson and raises the American

flag for the first time over an
Arizona site.

1848 A.D.	Treaty of Guadalupe Hidalgo is signed.
1853 A.D.	James Gadsden is sent to Mexico to negotiate a new boundary between Arizona and Mexico.
1854 A.D.	Gadsden Treaty is ratified.
1855 A.D.	Camels introduced into the Southwest.
1856 A.D.	United States flag raised over Tucson, as U.S. dragoons take formal possession of the Old Pueblo.
1861 A.D.	Sixty-eight Americans convene in Tucson and formally declare Territory of Arizona for the Confederacy.
1862 A.D.	Jefferson Davis signs act of Confederate Congress establishing Arizona as a Confederate territory.
1862 A.D.	Confederacy take possession of Tucson in February and, in April, Union and Confederate troops skirmish in Picacho Pass in only Civil War engagement fought on what is now Arizona soil.
1863 A.D.	President Lincoln signs into law the Territory of Arizona, making it

	a separate territory from New Mexico and appoints territorial officers.
1864 A.D.	Kit Carson defeats the Navajos at Canyon de Chelly and removes them to Bosque Redondo Reservation in New Mexico.
1864 A.D.	Territorial capital established at Prescott.
1864 A.D.	Mojave, Yavapai, Yuma, and Pima Counties created.
1865 A.D.	Last Confederate field army surrenders at Durham's Station.
1867 A.D.	General George Crook forces surrender of Hualapai, Tonto, and Yavapai Indians.
1868 A.D.	Territorial capital removed to Tucson.
1869 A.D.	John Wesley Powell begins exploring the Grand Canyon by boat.
1875 A.D.	Pinal County organized from parts of Maricopa, Pima, and Yavapai Counties.
1877 A.D.	Territorial capital returns to Prescott.
1877 A.D.	Ed Schieffelen discovers silver at Tombstone.
1880 A.D.	Southern Pacific arrives in Tucson. City of Phoenix is incorporated.

1889 A.D.	Territorial capital moved to Phoenix.
1900 A.D.	Railroad Brotherhoods become Arizona's first effective unions. Arizona population at 122,931.
1905 A.D.	Arizona's mining unions become dominated by the Industrial Workers of the World.
1906 A.D.	Arizona voters overwhelmingly reject joint statehood with New Mexico.
1908 A.D.	Grand Canyon established as a national monument.
1910 A.D.	President Taft approves measure that enables Arizona to elect members of convention to draw up constitution of Arizona as separate state.
1911 A.D.	Roosevelt Dam, world's highest masonry dam, dedicated.
1912 A.D.	Arizona admitted to the Union as forty-eighth state.
1917 A.D.	Vigilantes and Home Guard crush miners' unions by wholesale deportations.
1920 A.D.	Population hits the 334,162 mark.
1924 A.D.	Southwestern National Monuments Office is created.
1928 A.D.	Coolidge Dam is completed.
1930 A.D.	Population reaches 435,573.

1935 A.D.	Boulder Dam officially opened by President Franklin D. Roosevelt.
1936 A.D.	Hoover Dam (Boulder) dedicated by President Roosevelt.
1940 A.D.	Population rises to 409,261.
1955 A.D.	Population estimated at one million.
1964 A.D.	Senator Barry Goldwater is the Republican Party candidate for President.
1984 A.D.	Population estimated in excess of three million.
1985 A.D.	Central Arizona Project delivers water to state's interior.

BIBLIOGRAPHY

Anderson, Doherty Daniels. *Arizona Legends* (Phoenix, 1991).

Annerino, John. *Adventuring in Arizona* (San Francisco, 1996).

Bancraft, Hubert Howe. *History of Arizona and New Mexico 1530–1888* (Albuquerque, 1962).

Bolton, Herbert Eugene. *Rim of Christendom* (New York, 1960).

Bourke, John G. *On The Border With Crook* (New York, 1902).

Breakenridge, William M. *Helldorado* (Lincoln, 1992).

Carmony, Neil B. ed. *Apache Days and Tombstone Nights: John Clum's Autobiography* (Silver City, NM, 1997).

Cooke, Philip St. George. *The Conquest of New Mexico and California in 1846–1848* (Chicago, 1964).

Coolidge, Dane. *Arizona Cowboys* (Tucson, 1984).

Corle, Edwin. *The Gila* (Lincoln, 1951).

Cremony, John C. *Life Among the Apaches* (Glorieta, NM, 1868).

Dobynes, Henry F. *Spanish Colonial Tucson* (Tucson, 1961).

Dutton, Bertha P. *American Indians of the Southwest* (Albuquerque, 1990).

Fireman, Bert M. *Arizona: Historic Land* (New York, 1982).

Frazier, Donald S. *Blood and Treasure, Confederate Empire in the Southwest* (Texas A&M University, 1995).

Gressinger, A. W. *Charles D. Poston – Sunland Seer* (Globe, AZ, 1961).

Harte, John Bret. *Tucson Portrait of a Desert Pueblo* (Woodland Hills, CA, 1980).

Herring, Patricia Roche. "The Silver of El Real de Arizonac," *Arizona and the West, Vol. 20, No. 3.* (Tucson, 1978).

James, Harry C. *Pages From Hopi History* (Tucson, 1990).

Johnson, Paul. *A History of Christianity* (New York, 1995).

Kessell, John. *Friars, Soldiers and Reformers: Hispanic Arizona and the Sonora Mission Frontier 1767–1856* (Tucson, 1976).

Lake, Stuart N. *Wyatt Earp, Frontier Marshall* (Cambridge, MA, 1931).

Lucy, Beth/Stowe, Noel, eds. *Arizona at Seventy-Five* (Tucson, 1987).

Manje, Juan Mateo. *Unknown Arizona and Sonora* (Tucson, 1954).

McCarthy, Gary. *Grand Canyon* (New York, 1996).

McCarty, Kieran. *Desert Documentary* (Tucson, 1976).

McCool, Grace. *Gunsmoke: The True Story of Old Tombstone* (Tucson, 1990).

Milner, Clyde A., et al. eds. *The American West* (New York, 1994).

Officer, James E. *Arizona, 1536–1856* (Tucson, 1987).

Paré, Madeline Ferrin. *Arizona Pageant* (Tempe, AZ, 1975).

Peplow, Edward H. *History of Arizona, Vol. II* (New York, 1958).

Powell, Donald M. *The Peralta Grant: James Addison Reavis and the Barony of Arizona* (Oklahoma, 1960).

Powell, Lawrence Clark. *Arizona* (New York, 1976).

Sheridan, Thomas E. *A History of the Southwest* (Tucson, 1998).

——. *Arizona, A History* (Tucson, 1995).

Shoumatoff, Alex. *Legends of the American Desert* (New York, 1997).

Spicer, Edward H. *Cycles of Conquest* (Tucson, 1997).

Thrapp, Dan L. *The Conquest of Apacheria* (Oklahoma, 1967).

Trimble, Marshall. *Arizona: A Cavalcade of History* (Tucson, 1990).

——. *Arizona: A Panoramic History of a Frontier State* (Garden City, 1977).

——. *In Old Arizona* (Phoenix, 1993).

——. *Roadside History of Arizona* (Missoula, 1986).

Wagnorer, Jay J. *Arizona Territory 1863–1912* (Tucson, 1980).

Weber, David. *The Spanish Frontier in North America* (New Haven, 1992).

Wyllys, Rufus K. *Arizona: The History of a Frontier State* (Phoenix, 1950).

Arizona, Federal Writers Project. Original work by Ross Santee, ed. by Joseph Miller (New York, 1956).

WPA Guide to 1930s Arizona (Tucson, 1940).

ABOUT THE AUTHOR

Patrick Lavin was born in County Roscommon, Ireland. An avid history enthusiast, he spends his retirement years researching history and writing non-fiction books and articles. His works include *The Celtic World: An Illustrated History 700 B.C. to the Present* (Hippocrene Books) and *Celtic Ireland: Roots and Routes.* and *Thank You Ireland*, a compilation of success stories about the Irish in North America (co-authored with Irish-Canadian, Frank Keane).

Patrick is a graduate of California State University, Northridge and is retired from a career with the United States Government. He resides in Tucson, Arizona.

INDEX